OATH OF ALLEGIANCE

Copyright © 2014 Fred Oldenburg

Fred Oldenburg has asserted his right under the Copyright, Design and Patents Act, 1988 to be identified as the author of the work.

All rights reserved. No part of this publication may be reproduced, stored in a retrieval system, or transmitted in any form or by any means without prior written permission, nor be otherwise circulated in any form of binding or cover other than that in which it is published and without similar conditions being imposed on the subsequent purchaser.

ISBN-13: 978-1495375262
ISBN-10: 1495375269

OATH OF ALLEGIANCE

a Soldier's Story

FRED OLDENBURG

About the Author

Fred Oldenburg joined the Army in 1988 as an adult soldier. After basic training he joined his parent unit, 2nd Battalion, The Royal Anglian Regiment, where he served 23 of his 24-year military career. He served in many countries including numerous tours in Northern Ireland, Iraq, Afghanistan, Kuwait, Saudi Arabia, as well as exercises and training in the USA, Canada, Norway, France, Kenya, Brunei, Belize, Bermuda, Jamaica, Poland, Jordan, Cyprus, Germany and the UK.

He rose through the ranks to Warrant Officer Class Two (WO2) before leaving the military in September 2012 and starting work as the training Warrant Officer with the Bermuda Regiment. He retired from the Bermuda Regiment in October 2013 and presently lives with his wife in Gloucestershire, England.

Acknowledgements

Special thanks to my good friend Bruce Crowther, without whom this book would never have been more than a gathering of random badly worded memories; and my wife Catherine who gave me the strength and motivation to continue with this project when I lost direction.

To all my friends and acquaintances over my 24 years in the military. Too many to name but all have contributed in one way or another, ensuring I will always look back over my time served with pride.

Dedication

I dedicate this book to my mother, Brenda Oldenburg, taken from us too soon. Never far from our thoughts, always in our hearts.

Fred Oldenburg

PROLOGUE

AS WE APPROACHED KABUL the captain told us to buckle in and don our helmets and body armour. He then proceeded to drop the cumbersome C130 aircraft out of the sky groundward with the grace of a falling rock. This was to make it harder for any would-be arsehole to take a pot-shot at the aircraft as it came in to land. All I knew was my testicles were lodged in my throat and I was sure we were going to plough into the ground. At what appeared to be the last possible moment the pilot pulled the plane out of its kamikaze death dive and the wheels smashed into the tarmac at Kabul International Airport with a weighty thud followed by an intense whine as the turboprop engines went into reverse thrust bringing us to an abrupt halt.

We were ushered out of the aircraft and into the night heat and stench that was Kabul. Although I was overjoyed to be alive the foetid heated smell that greeted us was awful, and even after four months there I would never get used to it. This was worse than Jordan; and God knows that was bad. The buildings were for the most part destroyed by the American bombardment during the early part of the war but the local people still lived in the shells that were left. The sewerage system, long ago ruined, was spilling its contents into the main roads and the heat of the day then dried it into a fine layer of faeces dust. The small amount of wind that managed to blow in from the towering surrounding mountains then stirred up this fine dust and gave the air above Kabul a dirty, sickly yellow tinge. Many guys over the next few months would become ill or suffer from the effects of asthma from inhaling what was in essence, shit.

The one thing that was evident straight away was the amount of people that were everywhere. Women, children and men, all in rags and all attracted to Kabul by some unknown promise. There were beggars at every street corner and stray dogs wandered the place in hungry packs.

Unemployment was over eighty percent and there did not seem to be much promise here for anything other than disease, poverty and an early grave among the many thousands scattered along the surrounding hillsides.

The people could not understand why we were here and we could not understand why they didn't want all the freedoms and life styles we enjoyed back home. They were a simple and proud people who wanted very little in their lives; as long as their families were safe and their religion and culture were not insulted they were happy. I remember asking one of the interpreters why they all lived in this squalor and his reply was, it was Allah's will they lived as they did. This was a view they took on life as a whole, and it became apparent from something that happened a few weeks into the tour.

One day our patrol brought us to a small village not far from our camp. We were on foot patrol checking for possible areas from where the insurgents could launch mortars or rockets. As we came out of an alleyway that led to an open area of marshy ground I stopped short and brought the remainder of the platoon to a halt in all-round defence. To our front and off to the side of a large pond were two people, one an elderly man and the other a wailing woman. They were looking towards the centre of the pond where a small motionless body lay face down in the water. I sent my lead scout and medic into the pond, which was knee-deep, to pull the body out. It turned out to be a small girl aged about ten. She was blue, cold and very dead. When we debriefed the interpreter later he told us the girl had been in the water for about an hour by the time we got there and the parents had arrived shortly after she had gone in. When I asked the interpreter why they hadn't gone in to save their own daughter he said simply that it was Allah's will that the girl was to die that day.

What a crock of shit!

CHAPTER ONE

I was that which others cared not to be. I went where others feared to tread and did what others failed to do. I asked nothing from those who gave nothing, and accepted the thought of loneliness or death should I fail. I have seen the fog of war, the face of battle, felt the chill of fear, the spirit of victory, the pain of defeat. . . I lived in times others would say best forgotten. However, at the very least, in later days, I will be able to say with the greatest of pride, that I indeed was a soldier. - author unknown

MY MEMORIES OF MY father from the earliest times were of a big and hard man. He had left school in his early teens and followed his father's footsteps to the sea. He first went onto the fishing boats that operated out of Amsterdam docks and then a few years later onto the lifeboats. He loved the sea and after a few years around the coast of Holland, which isn't that big, he grew restless and joined the merchant navy to explore places further afield. It was in the mid-1960s that Dad joined the supply ships that were working among the booming oil and gas industry in the North Sea. It was while re-supplying the oil rigs that he decided he wanted to work on them; it was also during this time that my father met my mother.

My mother, Brenda, was born a Scouser but had been raised on the Isle of Man. She may have been small in stature but what she lacked in physical size she more than made up for in character. She was a kind and caring woman and during my rebellious childhood I am under no illusions that she stopped my father from dishing out some serious beatings on many occasions; and for just cause. At the time they met Dad was working on the ship that supplied the pirate radio vessel, Radio Caroline, broadcasting off the coast of the Isle of Man. It was during a re-supply visit to Ramsey port on the island that my dad met my mother's brother, Dougie, who arranged a blind date between my mum and dad, probably for a bet, but it ended up going really well and despite the fact that my old man couldn't speak English and Mum didn't even know where Holland was on a map, they hit it off. However it happened, they fell in love and within a few weeks Mum had moved across to Amsterdam where they were wed. My dad started work on the river barges and my mum moved in with my dad's parents and within a year I was born.

For most people, Christmas is a time of celebration and overindulgence. For my mother in the wee small hours of Christmas morning, 1968, after twelve hard hours of labour, I came onto the scene. The list of names my parents had compiled for my arrival read like something from an ancient manuscript, with Jesus head of the list. I kid you not! Thank God the alcohol had worn off by the time they wrote my name into the Birth Register, and I became Frederick, after my dad. It was a short reprieve. As is common practice in Holland, Frederick was shortened to Ferry, which later on, as a piss-take, became Fairy. By the time I was twelve, I'd had enough and demanded that Fred was shorter and manlier.

It was in my first year that my parents decided that family life would be better if we all moved onto the river barge with my dad and travelled together. Not that I could remember but by all accounts they were good years, if not a bit lonely, as there were no other kids around, just a scruffy old black retriever to play with. That was soon to change though when my sister decided to join the family, weighing in at a massive ten and a half pounds. Michelle would eat anything in sight, including my food if I wasn't quick enough. My world as I knew it had collapsed. For the previous two years of my life I had been the centre of attention for my parents, and even the scruffy dog, but now a little fat person had moved in on my turf and I wasn't happy. I felt like last year's presents, unwanted and shoved in the corner.

Life on the barge was a bit cramped for the four of us now and my dad decided to move us all back to the Isle of Man. He started work on the oil rigs in the North Sea and we moved into a three-bedroom house just outside Ramsey. Life was good and we wanted for nothing as the money Dad was bringing in was very good. It was around this time that I first recall not seeing very much of my dad; he would go away for anything from two weeks to three months at a time, with irregular bits of time at home here and there. He had become a stranger to my sister and I but we would always look forward to his homecomings, as he would bring presents and laughter, and the house would be turned upside down from the normal routine. As well as the presents there would be holidays and meals out, but with it came my father's discipline. He was old school and as long as we lived under his roof we abided by his rules. It took me eighteen years before I fully understood and respected what he was all about.

My mum was no pushover but she had the cool head and the harsh tongue whereas my dad had his presence and his right hand. He tried not to rock the boat, so to speak, when he came home, but if we backchatted him or my mum or misbehaved then he would step in, never a pleasant thing. He was never cruel or malicious; he was just a man who didn't take any crap from my sister and me. From as young as I can remember I would look up at that big lump of a man that was my dad and dream of the day that I would be bigger and stronger than him. I'm sure in the back of his mind it pushed him a bit also, to make sure that that day wouldn't happen for a long while yet.

My father also brought to the household stories of faraway places, people and different cultures. We spent the years ahead moving with my dad from one country to another. Trinidad and Tobago, the Canary Islands, Malta, America and even Iran, to name but a few. The time we spent in these countries was dependant on how long the oil rig remained on location. Sometimes it would be for six months, other times we would stay put for a year or more. For Mum and Dad it was time spent together they would normally not have, but for my sister and me it meant we didn't form any long-term friendships, and had constant upheaval and the need to play catch-up during school years.

When I was eleven years old my dad moved us all to Singapore where we spent an amazing four years while he worked on an oil platform operating off the coast of Malaysia and Indonesia for an American firm called Reading and Bates. He had been promoted with the move and the money he was pulling in meant the lifestyle we were living was something most could only dream of. We lived in a big three-bedroom house with a swimming pool, and even as snotty-nosed kids my sister and I knew we had it good. My dad's shift pattern was a month on the rigs and a month at home, which is still six months away a year, but we were more grown up now and understood it better. My sister and I went to an American school on the other side of the island called Ulu Pandan American School, which meant an epic three and a half hour return bus journey every day, but it was worth it. The campus was massive and catered for all ages of students from five years old up to eighteen, and had over five thousand students. It was by far the best school that I ever went to. It was during my time here that I developed a deep-founded interest for sport, it was a way of life for the American kids and the variety of sport on offer was almost limitless.

After about a year living in Singapore my parents decided to buy a 52-foot ketch-rigged yacht and duly moved us all on board. It was an old hand-built mahogany vessel that screamed out for a hell of a lot of tender loving care, but nevertheless we moved on board and she became our new home. For the first few months life on board was new and exciting but as the rainy season set in the cramped conditions and the leaky deck, that became even more leaky after a few hours, normally about two in the morning, was taking its toll. To earn my pocket money of ten dollars a week I had a series of chores. These included daily trips back and forth to the sailing club as we were moored about 200 metres off shore. I would trundle back and forth with a little inflatable dinghy stacked high with full rubbish bags and empty water jerry cans to be refilled, and on Saturday mornings I would have to jump over the side of the yacht and scrub the green algae from the water line. This was fine for a while as I loved the sea and loved swimming, but then I saw the film *Jaws*. My imagination took over and any time I took to the water and couldn't see the bottom I visualized sharks waiting in the depths for me. I was such a skinny little shit then I'm sure any shark would have found more use for me as a toothpick than a meal.

The two main characters I hung around with back then were Dave and Nick, an American and a Filipino kid. Their fathers both worked for oil companies and we would spend most of our free time together messing around and generally getting up to no good. Even back then, Singapore was an amazing place; ultramodern and yet around every corner and back street was a bit of old China, and lots of other bits of Asia. The three of us would meet up every weekend down in Changi village with our pocket money, buy our supplies and head for the sailing club. It was here we kept our two-man kayaks; we had come across them at a disused water sports park a few months earlier. With lies to our parents, saying that we were staying at each other's houses, we would load up our stuff and head for the outlying islands that dotted the coast of Singapore. Once at the islands we would head up the rivers and into the mangrove swamps where we would set up camp for the weekend. They were fun times, full of adventure and mischief; we grew up fit and strong and life was good. Most of the islands still had ruins and bunker systems left behind by the Japanese from the Second World War and these became our bases where we would launch our missions into the jungle. The Dutch, American and Filipino navies re-enacted many battles back then.

On Sunday late afternoons we would paddle back to the sailing club and head home to explain our cuts and bruises, but unable to hide our smiles.

It was about six months into living on the yacht that I gained the attention of one of the local Asian lads that lived in the area. It started off as stern glares and the occasional comment passed at me in Chinese but one day as I got off the bus from school he was waiting for me. He was lean and had a determined and cruel look to him. When he hit me I didn't even see it coming. He walked away happy and triumphant and I went home beaten and depressed. So much for my first fight. Well, it wasn't really much of a fight; I didn't even get a punch in.

If we were not canoeing off the islands we would jump on our BMX bikes and head into Singapore city. It was a hubbub of activity and we would spend hours looking through the local markets and seeing what trouble we could get into. Our best pastime was to use the local population as moving targets for our home-made catapults and wadded paper bullets. No one was spared and when fired from a moving bus the impact was painful. It was during one of our outings that the local police spotted and cornered us. Our escape plan was pathetic and I was caught. My arrogant attitude was soon crushed by the police sergeant's backhander across my face but the pain of the copper's slap was nothing compared to my father's welcome when he picked me up from the police station later that evening.

Attitudes in Singapore, as in many other places in the world, are different in many ways from our western ways, especially to their religion and customs, which also included their outlook on death. It was while exploring the back streets of China Town in downtown Singapore that I first came across death first hand. Of course I knew what death was. I had seen my dad cry for the first time when he received the news that his dad had died. Death was something delivered by phone and not a visual thing and yet as I wandered down a back road there was this old woman laid out for display, and very much dead. She looked peaceful and there was no grimace of pain etched into her face as I had thought death would bring, it was if she were sleeping. As I put my hand onto her arm I withdrew it as if I had been stung, she was as cold as a piece of marble. It would be many more years before I would feel that coldness again and then it would be my own father.

It was also while in Singapore that I first started windsurfing. When we had moved onto the yacht there was an old windsurfer strapped to the side railing, it was about fifteen feet long and must have been a prototype for the first aircraft carrier. It was huge. With patience not being one of my main virtues in life it took me nearly two years of raging temper tantrums before I could sail in a straight line and turn around to get back to my starting point. Little did I realize back then that learning to windsurf would pay dividends later on in my life. I still remember the day I got stranded in the busy water channel drifting towards Malaysia. With no wind in which to sail I saw the head of a sea snake break the surface of the water to my front and head for me. To say I shit myself would be an understatement. Sea snakes regularly come up for air but to my eyes it was after me and I frantically waved for help to my parents who were sunbathing on the deck of the yacht. To them, I was waving, as kids do, and they went back to soaking up the tropical rays on the deck. To me, I was living the last thirty seconds of my life on earth. As it got to within ten metres of the board the snake dipped its grotesque head and dived under the surface carrying on with its leisurely lifestyle, not interested in petrified me. My legs went weak and I sank down onto the board, thankful to be alive.

All good things come to an end, and Singapore was no exception. The contract for the oil rig came to an end in 1984 and my dad made plans to move the family to Gran Canaria, which is the largest of the Canary Islands, just off the northwest coast of Africa. Again we moved into a large house, this one in the north of the island. My sister started in the British school and I was put into the American International School, which suited me down to the ground. My dad was working off the African coast and for the next couple of years we settled into life in the sub-tropical sun. I was never the greatest academic, and I am sure my parents spent many a sleepless night rereading my report cards and wondering what would become of their brain-dead son. In the meantime I made friends with a few American guys at the school, most of them older than me, and was introduced to the world of motorcycles. Most of the group I hung around with had their own machines, ranging from screaming little 50cc chicken chasers to 250cc scramblers. We did not need driving licences to ride around on the roads out there, and with a good tail wind, a steep hill, and a banshee yell we could reach speeds of 70 mph. When you are young and fearless, as we were, our bikes were flat out at every opportunity; how I never met my end on my little 50cc I will never know.

My school was only half an hour's ride away from our home and every day I would try and go that little bit faster and brake that little bit later into the corners. The neighbours must have hated the ratty screech coming from my redlining engine, but to me it was the purr of a Harley Davidson. Being part of the group brought with it a social life and it was through the lads that I was introduced to a girl called Natalia, a little Spanish thing, gorgeous and pretty. I on the other hand was a shy and nervous skinny wreck. I had witnessed first hand my dad with my sister's boyfriends and seen the look of terror on their faces as he questioned them on their intentions; there was no way I was going to be put through an embarrassing situation like that. Instead, I never mentioned that I had a girlfriend. I would make my excuses and meet her anywhere but at my home; she knew something was amiss but never questioned it much. Anyway, my shyness was banished soon after my sixteenth birthday as she led me down to the beach front on the Las Palmas strip and took my virginity. She didn't make me a man but I did have a Cheshire grin on my face that lasted a week.

Our little gang would bunk off school fairly frequently and head down to the sand dunes of Maspalomas beach. If you have never been there it is pretty spectacular; miles of rolling sand dunes stretching along the northern coast of Gran Canaria. We would head straight to our favourite area, which was the nudist section of the beach. It was there we could watch some very gorgeous young woman wandering up and down the beach. Unfortunately there were also a few monsters among them; in all, though, it was a good day out.

It was on a bunk off from school that I nearly lost my life whilst giving my cavalier approach to life a hefty kick up the arse. My mate Arturo and I were walking along a rocky section of the coast where there were some huge geysers that would shoot water around thirty metres into the air. As we passed between the geysers and the sea a large wave came in and forced the sea upwards, through the geyser pool from the underground tunnel and flooding the ledge we were on. As the wave retreated back to the sea we were sucked into the pool and then down through the tunnel. It happened so fast we could not react and with a quick breath we were forced under the water. The power of the sea was overwhelming and I felt my body being dragged and turned as it was sucked away from the shore. People say that their lives flash before their eyes during near-death experiences and I can vouch for that. I was probably only under the water for thirty or forty seconds but I saw flashes of my life, and vividly remember thinking I should have been nicer to my mother. I wished I'd told her I loved her that day. I reckon the Soft Fairy had come down to get me or something. As it was we were pushed up to the surface about twenty metres out to sea where the current then started to force us further away from the coast. With our adrenalin in overdrive we struck out for the shore and eventually were thrown upon the rocks, scratched and bruised, but alive. Later that day I went home and gave Mum a big hug, which brought about confused looks and questions as to what I had done wrong.

Approaching two years into living in Gran Canaria we again found ourselves on the move. My dad had changed oil rigs and we moved to

Great Yarmouth, Norfolk, England. I was enrolled into Duncan Hall Secondary School, which was a boarding school, but they also had day students. It was a culture shock coming from the American education system that I had been used to, and as I turned up for day one in my blazer and tie I felt like a fish out of water. As it was, it wasn't all that bad and I made some new friends and got stuck into my final year at school. My dad had always said he would pay for me to go to further education but my heart and my grades were not up to it; I didn't want to spend any longer than necessary in school. My thoughts for the first time turned to the army and what I would do once I decided to leave school. So much so that on one Saturday afternoon I made my way by train to Norwich city centre and sought out the Army Recruiting Office. My knowledge of all things military was zero, and as I passed the Royal Navy Recruiting Office I saw the advert for joining the Royal Marines and thought, what the hell, they're soldiers as well. I sailed through the initial paperwork and did a series of physical tests and passed with flying colours, but the recruiting sergeant told me that I should finish my O Levels (now GCSEs) and return with some educational qualifications. The forces have their scaled-down education system in place for those who need it, but to arrive with exam results in place saves a lot of time and hassle later on in your career. I left with promises that I would return once my exam results were given. Little did I realize that I would not revisit the military option until nearly two years later.

While at Duncan Hall School I was introduced to the game of rugby football for the first time in my life. I initially became a first team player for the school, and then was poached for the local senior side, the Broadlands Colts, with whom I trained twice a week, and played every Saturday during the rugby season. Until this time of my life I had never had much to do with alcohol, but as is the way with the rugby fraternity after every game I would end up getting leathered on two pints of cheap lager and then stagger home to bed. I tried to hide the fact that I had been drinking, but in hindsight I must have looked like a right twat, red-eyed, giggling and basically looking like a very pissed-out-of-my-head version of me. My parents never pushed the subject, I reckon they must have thought that I was old enough and ugly enough to decide for myself if I wanted a drink or not.

As it was, school was fast approaching exam time and decision time on whether to continue with my education or take that huge step into the big wide world. The thought of getting a job and making it on my own away from my parents' direct support scared the crap out of me, but I also knew that I didn't want to go to school any longer than I needed. I told my parents that I was going to quit school and get myself set up on a

Youth Training Scheme (YTS) in diesel mechanics, which was an apprenticeship with two days a week in college and the remainder on work experience with a local company.

I started work within a week with a firm called J.W. Munnings Plant Hire in Great Yarmouth, and that Friday brought home my first pay check. I was hooked. I had money in my pocket and even though it wasn't much, as far as I was concerned I was a millionaire. My dad bought me my first car, a Vauxhall Chevette, purple, old and a bit rusted, but it was mine and I loved it. Life was good. A couple of months into the YTS and I decided that I wanted more money, so gave my notice to the college and work and went looking for more lucrative earnings. Luckily enough, the firm wanted to keep me, and I ended up going full time onto their books. My pay packet jumped overnight from £35 a week to £150. It was 1987 and I had made it into the big league; well, in my head I had. My time with J.W. Munnings lasted a further eighteen months until I grew restless and knew there was something else out there for me. One weekend while shopping in Norwich I tried to find the Royal Navy Recruitment Office again, but instead stumbled onto the Army Recruitment Office. Not knowing any different, I went in and signed up for three years service for Queen and Country. I was told that if I was successful in completing basic training I would be shipped out to the Royal Anglian Regiment, the local infantry unit. My basic training started in just two months' time.

CHAPTER TWO

The ultimate measure of a man is not where he stands in moments of comfort and convenience, but where he stands at times of challenge and controversy. - Martin Luther King, Jr

As I stepped off the train at Royston, Kent, my heart was in my throat. To say I was nervous would be the biggest understatement in the world. Any more nervous and I would have shit my pants. A stocky corporal glared at us and read out our names, while ushering us onto a waiting four-ton truck. We were driven the short distance to Bassingbourne Barracks, which would be our home for the next five long months, and told we would be part of Falaise Platoon. All the training platoons were given the names of famous British battle honours and we were encouraged to learn all we could about them, with punishments given out if we could not recite dates and facts. Over the first few weeks we were taught everything from how to iron our uniforms, to wash and shave correctly, and, of course, drill. We were drilled constantly, until I dreamt about marching in my sleep. Throughout training and my full army career I never enjoyed drill. I know the reasoning behind it, but it never caught on with me and I always managed to get away with all but the basics throughout my time in the army. It was about week three when we were introduced to what was to be our personal weapon, the SA80 A1 5.56mm assault rifle. For somebody who had never fired or even handled a weapon before it was an eye opener. The loud crack and thump of the round being fired down the range made my heart race and for a while I wasn't sure that this is what I wanted to do. After a few weeks though I had become accustomed to my rifle and other weapons firing. I had come to love live firing days; this in my eyes was what being a soldier was all about.

My time in basic training, which was five months long, seemed to fly and as training progressed I changed with it. I was no longer the gawky unconfident teenager I used to be and as each hurdle was overcome new ones were set up and as they too were passed I became cocky, thinking there was nothing that I couldn't do. As a platoon we lived, slept and trained together. Each knowing the other's strong and weak points, each of us relying on the platoon to get us through all the hardships and the low points. The proudest day of my life up until that point was the six week passing off the square parade. This was where we were given our unit's berets and also our civilian clothing was returned to us. This was also where our families came down to watch us on the drill parade, and afterwards we could go home for a well-deserved long weekend, the first in six long gruelling weeks.

The return from our long weekend was also a turning point in our basic training; we were now thrown into real soldiering. The members of the platoon who had fallen by the wayside were remembered only by upturned beds on which were pinned names and drop-out dates. This was a timely reminder to the rest of us of the achievements we had made to get this far alone, and I have no doubt it was also a reason that a lot of us stuck it out when the going got tough, which it did a lot of the time. We spent less and less time in the relative comfort of the camp and more time out on the various training areas, honing our skills as infantry soldiers. Camouflage and concealment, weapon handling and section and platoon attacks were pounded into us until they became second nature. As we were constantly told, the reason we were practised in the same drills time and time again was so that when we were under fire for real, and the fear and adrenalin were coursing through our bodies, we wouldn't have to think; it would all come naturally. This would prove itself to be true many times over the next few years.

And just when you thought you had done all the training and exercises you needed to do, you would find yourself doing it all over again - but with live ammunition. The senses were now in overdrive as live rounds were buzzing left and right of you, the hairs on the back of your neck rigid as you bounded forward with troops to the rear laying down suppressive fire support metres away from you. It was more than trust. It was giving over to the fact that you knew that those around you knew their job and wouldn't let you down. The training staff were finding it harder to rein us in; we did things ourselves without always asking first. This wasn't us being rebellious; this was what we were trained to do. The

British Army had realized that the best type of soldier is a thinking soldier and openly encouraged soldiers to make a decision without always asking permission. Better to try and fail than to not try at all.

As our time at Bassingbourne came to an end we were all called in to speak with the relevant training directing staff and confirm our forward movement to our respective units. As I was recruited in Norwich I was pencilled in to join the First Battalion of the Royal Anglian Regiment, which was based in Gibraltar. My interest however had wandered towards the Second Battalion by now, as they were about to deploy on operations to Northern Ireland. I had no idea why the British Army was deployed there, and to tell the truth, I didn't care. I had seen the pictures and heard the stories on the news and I wanted to go there and experience soldiering in Northern Ireland first hand. I wanted the rush of operations and combat.

The Second Battalion of the Royal Anglian Regiment, also known as the Poachers, was based in the small German market town of Celle. This was in the north of Germany about half an hour's drive away from Hanover. I had managed to get a lift from my training corporal, Mick Baker, who had filled me full of stories from the battalion and was probably another of the reasons I had decided to change from the First to Second Battalion, as well as the Northern Ireland tour. Again, my heart was in my throat as we drove through the front gates of Trenchard Barracks, home of the Poachers. I was to be a part of 1 Platoon of A Company, one of the rifle companies. The basic breakdown of an infantry company is three rifle platoons, each of twenty-eight men, and a smaller contingent, company headquarters. I was the red-arse new boy.

My new weapon now became a General Purpose Machine Gun (GPMG). It was the heaviest platoon weapon and because it was so heavy nobody wanted to carry it; except new guys, like me, who didn't have a choice. I didn't mind it all that much as I loved fitness and it was a gung ho macho bit of kit. The battalion was starting on its pretour training and no sooner had I joined them than I was off to Sennelager Training Centre to conduct an intense build-up package of exercises and field firing that would bring us up to the standards needed to deploy on operations to the volatile and dangerous area of West Belfast, Northern Ireland.

As I approached the gates of 'Tin City', a replica urban training village where the platoon was operating for the next seven days, I had not yet met the remainder of my platoon. Once more, my heart was in my throat. There was a layer of smoke hanging over the camp as I moved across the helicopter landing pad towards the briefing room. Now, camouflaged, tired faces stared at me and I felt alone and completely out of my depth.

These were real soldiers who had seen combat and looked the part. How could I match what these guys already knew? I was briefed on the situation on enemy forces and what was expected of me for the next week and the remainder of the training before I was taken to my section and bunked down for the night.

As it was, joining the battalion at this stage was probably the best thing that could have happened to me. All the hassle of being a new guy that you normally get back in the chilled atmosphere of camp was dispensed with and you were accepted into your sections quickly, and with little fuss. These people knew that in the next few weeks we would be on the streets of Northern Ireland and would have to cover each other's backs in life and death situations. Tin City was like nothing I had ever seen, done or imagined. They had you locked up in this small village for seven days and in that time they hit you with every conceivable situation you might encounter while deployed. It was fast and furious and the training was as real as they could make it without being there.

That same day I lined up with my section for a routine foot patrol and as the camp gates opened I ran like a man possessed, out into the village for the first time. This was it, make or break. My worst fear was that I would let my comrades down and fall short of the standard expected of me. As we came around one of the many side streets of the village we were met by a large crowd of approximately twenty people all chanting, "down with the British" and "long live the IRA". There were only four of us in our team or 'Brick', as we knew it by. We were part of a twelve-man team and the other two Bricks were out of sight of us but from our patrol brief we knew them to be forward and right of our position and in one of the other side streets. The scenario had been to move forward and check all activity around one of the pubs, to show a presence and to let the local population know the British Army were around the estate. I kept telling myself this was just training and nothing was going to happen to us but the people coming towards us were definitely pissed, and they looked genuinely angry with us. The civilian population (Civpop) that were used on these exercises were drafted in from other military units around the area and the unit facing us now were a bunch of Jocks who had recently completed their tour of Belfast. Civpop was considered a good number to be on and to make it all the more realistic they were allowed to drink and in fact were very drunk. Each person was given a character and they were to stay in their role throughout the exercise. They had with them their senior non-commissioned Officers (NCOs), who were keeping a stand-back approach with them in case things got too out of hand. The crowd had now doubled in number and as we faced up to them our other two teams closed in from the flanks for added support.

The first indication that the ante had escalated was a brick smashing into the guy's helmet to my right. He stumbled but steadied himself and remained standing. There was a banshee type yell and then the crowd rushed us. The first team to break away withdrew twenty metres, then turned to give us fire support with their baton guns as we turned and ran past them to the next bound before turning and forming a base line to giving fire support to them. We bounded like this for two more street junctions, the bricks and crowd in hot pursuit. I had received a stinging blow from a brick to my thigh and one to my shoulder and my lungs felt as if they were on fire. If I thought this was bad there was worse to come. We had been joined now by the Quick Reaction Force (QRF) from camp, and with them they had brought armoured vehicles that had blocked off the roads around us to stop the crowds from outflanking us. The base line was now held by soldiers with six-foot shields and others, with smaller four-foot shields, carrying wooden baton sticks. These were snatch squads, and when the baton gunners fired their plastic bullets and a rioter went down they would rush out from the protection of the six-foot shields and drag them back to a waiting police or army armoured Land Rover, parked to our rear.

As the bricks and the crowd intensified the first of the petrol bombs came over our base line; I couldn't believe what I was seeing. There were people on fire being put out by fire extinguishers and blankets and stretcher bearers taking away various other casualties from both sides. This was complete mayhem. The order eventually came across that we were to advance and clear the streets of all rioters. The vehicles would sound their horns and drive towards the rioters, twenty metres at a time, with us running behind in shielded walls. It was hard work and after what seemed like forever and then some, the crowds cleared and the directing staff ordered us back to our fortified base for a hot debrief.

Everything we did in the village was recorded on film and as we sat in the debriefing cinema the whole incident was replayed for all to see with comments being levelled at anyone who did anything good or bad; there was nowhere to hide.

"Who was that dick head cowering behind that wall?"

A hand would be raised in embarrassment and the directing staff would lay into him.

"If that were for real you would be dead, you idiot."

"Well done to that team."

"Who the fuck is that?"

All you could think of on the debrief sessions was, please don't have a go at me.

There was no respite during the week everyone spent in Tin City. After our time there we walked out like zombies. I could understand what they were trying to do but I couldn't help but think how it would not be possible to do this for six months. In our time in Tin City we had been shot at, blown up on foot patrols and in vehicles, mortared in camp numerous times and had enough rioting to realize that if this happened for real we would be in for a real fight just to survive. I left there with my head all over the place. I believed that I had done well enough and proved myself within my section. I was always being told to change my fire positions and spread out or close up but it was experience I lacked, not soldiering ability.

The training now changed direction to that of theory lessons, and then when taught you would go out and do it practically on the ground. The subjects ranged from First Aid, radios, weapons training and patrolling, to suspect recognition. The learning curve was steep but I loved it. This is what I expected being in the army to be about. The final part of our build-up training package was a week's live firing. Everything I had done in basic training was nothing compared to this. The ranges were intense and demanding, think before you fire and when you do open fire, shoot to kill. Maximum violence in the shortest amount of time. If you wanted to live, then your speed and aggression was what was going to save your life. Trust your fellow soldiers and they will trust you, work together and you will return from Northern Ireland alive and in one piece. Sounded good to me. I liked my legs, and body for that matter, in one piece. Training was now complete and before we deployed we were given a fortnight's leave. My parents and sister had in the meantime moved to Spain, so with sun lotion packed as well as a bag full of war stories off I went.

The brief relaxing respite over, it was back to business. Flying into RAF Aldergrove, Belfast, I couldn't believe how big the place was. There were helicopters and planes of every description everywhere. Armoured vehicles and soldiers moved about with purpose, and the feeling was intense. We were offloaded from the Hercules transport aircraft and then loaded onto civilian vans. Contact drills were explained to us in case there was an incident en route and then we were driven down the back roads towards West Belfast. We had weapons but no ammunition and everyone just sat there in between all the bags and prayed nothing happened. We were to be based at Fort Whiterock, which was a small mortar-hardened outstation located at the foot of the Black Mountains that dominated the landscape of West Belfast. After the build-up training we had received prior to deployment I expected a war zone to surround us. What we got instead was a scene that was identical to any place in England. Housing estates - some nice, others not so nice - lay before us. As the gates opened on that first patrol I ran like my life depended on it and waited with bated breath for the inevitable barrage of automatic fire and exploding bombs that would hit us. Instead we got nothing but indifference and a quiet hostility. People were shopping, driving and going about their daily routine as they would do back home. I did not understand the reason behind the Troubles. We had it explained to us but it didn't mean anything. I have no doubt if any one of us were in their shoes and soldiers were patrolling our streets, stopping us and kicking our doors down in the middle of the night, we would not be happy, and would probably also do something about it.

After the first few patrols it would have been easy to be lulled into a false sense of security had it not been for the fact that on day two of the tour one of our patrols was hit by a drainpipe bomb and our first fatality occurred. The Rock Bar, a well-known hangout for Republican terrorists, had been passed by one of our patrols. A couple of women were having a heated argument and as the patrol went to calm the situation down the women legged it and a device, hidden in the drainpipe attached to the pub, detonated, killing one of the patrol instantly. It made everyone realize straight away that these people meant business and if we were to leave this place alive we would have to be professional and alert all the time. Like everyone who has been on an Operational tour I must have passed a barrier in my life without even realizing it. This barrier was a mental acceptance that there was only so much you could prevent before things outside of your control took over. Every time we ran and darted left and right when leaving the main gate to throw off any would-be sniper or we hard-targeted past heavily-laden cars in case there was a hidden bomb inside, there was always that extra thought that something else could happen. To dwell on these things for long would drive you insane so you would put these thoughts to the back of your mind and just hoped that if the grim reaper came calling it would be a quick end. It may sound a bit morbid but it stopped the worry driving you crazy.

The hours we worked, like on all the tours I was to do, were long and hard, with sixteen-hour days being the normal routine. While on the tour we had numerous incidents, and others from the battalion suffered life-changing injuries. When we received our intelligence briefs every morning we were even told who had carried out these attacks, but unless they were caught in the act, or forensics proved it was them, we couldn't touch them. What we could do was put a covert and overt presence on the streets to catch them, and in a lot of cases we wanted them to have a go at us. It was every soldiers dream to kill one of the bastards; especially the ones we knew were the evil ones. Many nights we would lay up hidden outside houses or shops waiting for a terrorist (player) to turn up but ninety-nine percent of the time we would move back to camp cold, bleary eyed and disappointed. These guys had been doing this for twenty-five years and were not stupid. You couldn't move out of the gates of the camp without the locals phoning around and telling everyone the Brits were out on the streets.

On one patrol we became involved in the biggest crowd disorder we had while we were out there. There was a place just outside Fort Whiterock called Kelly's Corner, and it was the gathering place for all the teenagers and dropouts in the area. Many attacks on the security forces had been launched from this area. There was an off-licence, a Spar shop and a post office to collect their dole money from. Most days these idiots would just hang around there giving grief to some of the locals and wait for an army or Royal Ulster Constabulary (RUC) patrol to pass. If we were in vehicles we would just put our foot down and take the stones or anything else they could throw at us, but one day the Platoon Sergeant said we were to do a foot patrol through Kelly's Corner. We knew it was going to kick off but we didn't realize then just how much.

As we approached the shops the first of the teenagers spotted us and raised the alarm, bringing the rest of his mates instantly into the area. First there were just words shouted but this soon turned to a hail of stones raining down upon us. With our helmets and visors secured into position we advanced towards the small crowd. As with anything in Northern Ireland it didn't take long for word to get around that the Brits were here and anyone who had a grudge, which seemed to be everyone, came out for a fight; women included. The platoon's baton gunners were moved to the front of our advance and after a series of quick target indications were given to them pointing out the ring leaders within the crowd they let loose with a barrage of rubber bullets into the throng of people. We were trained to never fire the baton gun less than ten metres away from a target unless your life was in danger but as the crowd tried to rush us the loud bangs of the baton guns and the impact of our baton sticks against flesh became one. This had now gone from an orderly advance to an all-out scrap and although we had anti-sniper teams off to our flanks, in the middle it was just mayhem and violence. To have the fear of death with you and adrenalin pumping gave us the advantage and after what seemed like an eternity, but was probably only ten or fifteen minutes, the crowd broke and ran. As they fled the RUC arrived and followed up with their own brand of policing. These guys were brutal, but then again they had to be to fight these people.

Ireland came and went fairly quickly and to tell you the truth I quite enjoyed my six months there, I had become one of the boys and I had grown up. We were sent back to Celle, Germany, where we had to do three weeks work in camp before being let loose on three weeks well-earned leave. The three weeks in camp was supposed to chill you out a bit and get you used to being back in a normal environment, instead of going home and bringing the conflict with you to people who could never understand what you had seen or done. Did it work? I don't know, but it was a bloody good piss-up.

CHAPTER THREE

If you spend your whole life waiting for the storm, you'll never enjoy the sunshine. - Morris West

ONE OF THE THINGS I had already noticed with the army was that it was a drink culture. If you did well at something they would give you beer. If you had just battered some guy into submission in the boxing ring or had just finished the 400 metres in your best time you would be handed beer. The three weeks directly after our return from Ireland could only be described as a mass piss-up: BBQs, company parties and visits to breweries to name but a few. We would all head down to Hanover, which was about an hour away by train from Celle, and head straight for the red light district, with its strip bars and brothels. At this stage in my life I had never seen anything like this and as the older soldiers led a few of us younger ones down this alleyway we were told in no uncertain terms that if we didn't go through with their game we were in trouble. We came to this huge door and as they led us through one of the older lads took out his wallet and handed the doorman a wad of bills. We were then told to make our way down the alley which had been made up to look like a small street, with windows either side and large fat black women hanging out, beckoning us with their fat fingers.

With a fear I had not known since my first patrol in Northern Ireland months ago, I made my way down the centre of the aisle and tried to fend off the flailing hands with those behind me doing the same. I had managed to get about three windows down before I was hooked by a huge calloused black finger and dragged effortlessly through a window.

The room was quite nice, unlike the thing that stared at me with lustful eyes and a Jabba the Hut body. My first thought was to shoot her, but I had no rifle, then I thought I would start swinging, but she would probably leather me. I would have run, but my legs had gone weak. Instead, I let her grab me and have her evil way. I left shortly afterwards with the older lads pissing themselves laughing and the small group of us new guys wondering whether to call the police. This, as it turned out, was an initiation and the rest of the night was a blast. The night life of Hanover was great and for the rest of my time in Germany would be the place to go and party.

It wasn't all good times in Hanover though. A few of the lads and myself went down town one night shortly after getting back from Ireland and would remember it for a long time to come. We had done a pub crawl around the red light district already and thought we would head out to one of the many night clubs in the area. The one thing we had forgotten was the area we ended up in was a popular place for the local Turkish community. As we were having a quick snack in McDonald's I noticed a group of Turks watching us. In good British style I asked if they had a problem. One replied he did; he didn't like British soldiers. Well, to me that was a declaration of war and I duly informed him that after my Big Mac I was going to take him outside for a good thrashing. He smiled and said he and his mates would gladly meet us outside. I should have known we were in big trouble. As we squared up to them the biggest of them kicked me in the side of the head so fast I didn't see it coming, but was told later that I had blocked his foot well with my head. As I slid down the front of a large shop front window I saw the other lads being punched and kicked by a large number of Turks. I was picked up by two other Turks and the guy who had initially kicked me was reaching into his pocket. I was sure it was going to be a knife but what he pulled out instead was a set of stainless-steel knuckledusters and as they connected with my face I felt my nose break and my sight dim. The sound of fast-approaching German coppers was a godsend and as I held my bloodied face I made my way from the scene as fast as I could. I met my battle-scarred friends at the main train station where we did some makeshift repairs to our heads and continued with our night out knowing that the next day's hangover would be colossal.

After my post-tour leave it was back to work and the routine of life in an infantry battalion between operations. Our role in Germany at this time was to hold off the Soviet hordes if they crossed over the borders and swept through Europe. When we were crashed out, which was quite often, we would load up our battle stocks of ammunition and deploy to pre-set areas and dig in. It was hard and soul destroying work and as we stood there in our freezing trench positions in our nuclear and biological chemical (NBC) protection suits waiting for the advance of the Soviets I wondered how long they expected us to last. Apparently on the modern battlefield an infantry soldier had a life span of fifteen seconds. In this day and age little seemed to have changed from the First and Second World Wars; trench positions with soldiers standing around waiting. When the word came back stating it was an exercise we all gave a sigh of relief, filled in our trenches and headed back to camp.

There were also lots of sports and lots of conventional warfare-type exercises all over Germany and across to Canada. Oh, and lets not forget the beer and the women. Every weekend we would go somewhere new and most weekends we would meet someone new. German women liked British soldiers and British soldiers liked German women. It was about this time when one of my mates was approached by the camp padre and asked if, as a practicing Catholic, he would like to go on a military pilgrimage to Lourdes in France. He agreed and stitched me up by saying I was also a Catholic and would love to go. I bluffed my way with the padre and even though in reality I had no religious beliefs I was signed up and off we went. We were told to turn up at Hanover train station dressed in military working dress and not to bring anything loud or outrageous, so as not to upset the pilgrims. This to us meant shopping in Hanover and turning up wearing jeans and T-shirts with a duck on the front saying 'Duck Off' and 'I don't give a Duck'. No one said anything to us; hundreds of people were going and no one actually knew who we were or what group we were in anyway. We spent the next week doing our own thing and basically acting as if we were on some kind of beach holiday. The hotel lobby every morning would be packed with all the military groups dressed up in their best uniforms and my mate and I would pass through them in loud shorts carrying blow-up air beds heading for the beach down the road at Biarritz to many confused looks, but no comments. The craziest thing was that we were just private soldiers and none of the senior NCOs or officers ever questioned what the hell we were doing.

On one night I managed to find a dodgy little night club down one of the back streets and on entering found the place packed with a couple of hundred uniform-clad soldiers. It was like some crazy fancy dress gay bar. In the corner I noticed two of the very few females there so we went across and got stuck into trying our best to chat them up; it also helped to make us look non-gay. As my mate loved nothing better than to drop me in the shit, he thought tonight would be the ideal opportunity. Unbeknown to me, he had moved across to a group of twenty German Luftwaffe airmen, pointing across at me saying that they had insulted me by calling me an arsehole and stating I wanted to fight them all. They, being Germans, had apologized and said they had come here to worship God and did not want to fight and left. As my mate came back and told me what he had said I couldn't believe he had done it. If they had been British they would have come over and kicked my head in. The girls said we were mad and left us. I had to walk back to the room with my still smiling mate. What a result!

In our room we would trash it every morning, turning anything we could find upside down and flooding the bathroom. To us it was hilarious; to the room maids we must have been the biggest idiots they had ever had as guests. When some Jock guardsmen came to see us later that night in our room one of them had to use the toilet and noticed the towels were covered in brown stains. We explained it was from wiping up chocolate biscuits but when they saw the state of the room they thought we were some grotty animals. There was no point in arguing the case.

The one thing that stood out while we were there is how people's beliefs can be so strong. There were caves and caverns that had crutches and wheel chairs hanging from the ceilings from people who had apparently come here and been cured by the water that ran through these areas. I saw sick people being wheeled into these caves on hospital beds; this was their last chance at life, their last chance for a miracle. I know the mind is a strong thing but it was spooky and a bit unnerving to think this was the last desperate cry out for help from a lot of these people. I left my mate there to pray for his unborn baby back home and jumped onto the bus to Biarritz and the beach. The only things I was going to pray for were some topless chicks and a cloudless day.

One of the big sports within the battalion was boxing and the battalion had a proven track record in Germany and back in the UK for winning the Army Amateur Boxing Championships. Before you could box for your battalion though you had to prove yourself in the Inter-Company Boxing Competition held every year. The boxers put forward to represent their companies were a mixture of volunteers and a few hand-picked novices chosen by Company Sergeant Majors, who watched their companies milling. Now milling is not boxing, milling is where we were shepherded into the gymnasium and the doors locked behind us. The company boxing coach would pair everyone off with someone of equal weight and size. Then, after being gloved up, you would be put into a makeshift ring and told to beat the crap out of your opponent. Some people would refuse to fight and would find out as their opponent started hitting them that they were left with little choice but to defend themselves, while others would be physically sick with the thought of having to fight. Others would run and try to hide, most however would just look at the person opposite and start swinging like a madman. If someone went down or was being hurt the coach would step in to split it up. What they were after was guts and determination and in some exceptional circumstances, skill.

With me it was definitely not skill. I had never boxed before and I just started swinging and hoped that I would either connect with my opponent's head or beat him by sheer fitness and more punches on target. Whatever they saw in me, I was picked for the company boxing team and started six weeks gruelling boxing training. I have always loved fitness training but this took it to a new level. Six days a week we would run for miles with a lot of the heavier weights wearing black bin bags and extra sweat kit to get their weight down to something they hadn't been since they were ten years old. Thankfully, I never had to lose more than a few kilos here and there as they wanted me to fight at the heavier weights rather than drop down.

We would spar every day but twice a week we would be paired off and heavy spar, which is basically a real fight. You were expected to use all the skills you had been taught. If you left your guard down, you could expect to be dropped by your opponent. If the trainers thought you were going easy on each other or being lazy they would glove up and go a couple of rounds with you; never nice. I remember the first time I got cocky in the ring and asked one of the trainers to go a few rounds with me as I thought I was ready to step up. The guy came through the ropes with a smile on his face and I should have known what was coming. What ensued over the next few minutes brought me back down to earth with a crash. He was smaller than me and as I swung hopeless punches that connected with fresh air his punches were deadly accurate and fast. Before long, they called a halt to the very one-sided contest and I was told to go and clean my battered face. My ego hurt a hell of a lot more than my head. I took away a vital lesson from this though; that is, how looks can be deceiving and no matter how hard you think you are there is always someone bigger and faster - or in this case, smaller and faster.

The company boxing finals came around and over the period of a week we fought through a series of preliminary bouts with the winner progressing gradually to the finals. It was a hard, punishing and gruelling week but I won all my bouts and by Friday I was confidently waiting in the changing rooms to be called out for the final of the middleweight competition. My opponent had won this event for the last two years but I was confident. The whole gymnasium had been transformed into a huge arena with the regulation-sized ring taking centre stage. There were floodlights and company flags draped everywhere. Lights were dimmed and the battalion's band in all their flash kit led out each boxer to the theme of *Rocky*. The company's shouted their relevant boxer's name as he made the long, lonely walk to the ring. The atmosphere was electric. Even when I watch the old matches today I get a tingle up my spine.

As I made my way to the ring with the band ahead of me and the floodlights following my walk, that old friend, fear, was all over me like a bad rash. It's not the fear of being hurt though, it's the fear of making yourself look stupid in the middle of the ring, where there is nowhere to hide. There was 256 square feet of canvas with two individuals in front of a large crowd, in the glare of the floodlights, with nowhere to hide or run and only gloved hands to protect yourself. It was the loneliest place in the world and appeared to be no bigger than a matchbox. Officers and senior NCOs were separated and the remainder of the 700 soldiers from the battalion, all in their best service dress, were shouting encouragement. It was loud, it was hot. What the hell was I doing here? The bell sounded and all went quiet except for my heartbeat and then even that calmed. In the end I lost on points, but I did not embarrass myself so I was happy enough, and my company commander gave me an extra three week's leave, and a crate of beer. Great! I awoke the next day with what was either a life threatening concussion or a hangover from hell; I couldn't tell.

THOSE DAYS IN GERMANY were good times and the best of my army career. I was a private soldier with hardly any responsibilities except to be a soldier. I worked hard and I played hard. I was sent away on a French commando course that was run on the German/French border near a place called Baden-Baden. It was a three-week course with the French Foreign Legion leading it. There were Americans, Germans, Italians and us Brits, as well as lot of French conscripts and this was my first time working with other nation's armies. It was a cold and demanding three weeks but I enjoyed it and seriously thought about joining the legion. They were a very professional outfit and looked the part. On my return to the battalion I was given a "well done" on completing the course and sent away on more leave. My parents were still in Spain but had moved and so with a map of the area and an address I went to find them.

After leave, I put my name down for selection in the battalion's Langlauf cross-country skiing team, which was forming up for the army's winter ski season across Europe. I had never skied before but I loved fitness and travel and it was an opportunity to do both. There was a two-week selection period in camp and at the end of the intense fitness period I was chosen as the eighth person on the eight-man squad. The worst of the best? We skied in all the Army's competitions across France, Austria and Norway and although I was never in the running to win any silverware the experience was amazing. I was to the battalion team what Eddie the Eagle was for the British ski jump team, a crap skier who tried hard.

I remember sitting in a bar in France watching the world news when the Iraqi invasion of Kuwait was under way. America and the UK were massing on the borders, threatening to push across and expel the Iraqis from the region. Here I was, sitting in some bar in France with some young Frenchwoman and I was missing out on the action. I didn't have long to wait though as the next day the team was pulled out of the remainder of the competitions and called back to the unit for deployment to operations in the Gulf. We were off to war.

Or so I thought.

CHAPTER FOUR

The difference between a friend and an acquaintance is that I would lay down my life for a friend. I have lots of acquaintances, but not many friends. - author unknown

BACK AT CAMP THE place was in uproar. The battalion had been put on short notice to move to Saudi Arabia and we had three weeks to get everything sorted. The next day I was sent away to complete the fastest Heavy Goods Vehicle (HGV) course in history and then directly afterwards onto a Warrior Fighting Vehicle driver's course. The Warrior is the British Army's armoured fighting vehicle (AFV) which we still use today; it is rated as one of the world's top armoured vehicles and is an awesome bit of kit.

We arrived in Saudi Arabia and were sent to a huge American and British camp where we were to gather all our kit and equipment and await further instructions. The land war had already started and we expected to be ordered over the border any day. The heat was like nothing we had ever come across, all of our build-up training had been done in Germany in freezing temperatures and although it was early January it was stiflingly hot. All the men were given Nerve Agent Pre-Treatment Sets of tablets (NAP), which were taken as an aid in the event of a chemical attack by Saddam. Nuclear, Biological and Chemical (NBC) drills were carried out daily. This was the coalition's main fear; a chemical attack, which they expected would leave huge casualties on our guys. To counter this, we donned our NBC suits and practiced everything from eating and drinking drills to section attacks. It was hard, hot work, and many a man collapsed with the heat.

Eventually, we were called forward to the border with Kuwait and again halted, more exercises and live firing lay ahead of us. No sooner had we got to the border area than the peace treaty was signed after the 100-hour ground war had all but completely destroyed the once-powerful Iraqi Army. We were sent straight over the border and through Kuwait city and north to the border with Iraq. The destruction we came across on our move north was unbelievable. The small oil rich country of Kuwait, once a shining modern beautiful place, lay broken and ruined. The Iraqis, on knowing they were beaten, destroyed as much of this place as they could, almost as if saying that if we can't have it, then no one will. Most of the capped oil wells were set alight and the huge oil fields lay burning, leaving the area looking like a scene from hell. The black smoke billowing overhead coated the sky, blocking the sunlight and leaving the country in half-darkness. Buildings were destroyed and the Iraqi Army had looted and packed all they could carry on their retreat north to Iraq. But the American Air Force, circling over head like hawks, had taken revenge. The road and areas left and right of them as they had tried to flee were littered with the dead bodies of Iraqi soldiers. Vehicles of every description and all their stolen cargoes littered the landscape like a hastily abandoned market. The smell of death was everywhere. We drove onwards through these scenes and realized that there was no romance or adventure in modern warfare, there was only death. Lots of the dead had not even realized what had happened, burnt figures still sat clutching steering wheels, not realizing their next breath would be their last. Among the dead were the dogs, packs of hungry snarling animals feeding off burnt and mangled human remains, left where they had fallen. We would shoot these animals on sight, the fear of rabies far outweighing our love for dogs. We made our temporary home in a place called St George's Lines. This was a large complex that started life as an industrial estate and at the beginning of Iraq's invasion the Iraqi military had then used it as a camp and briefing area for future battle plans. The familiar mapping of Saudi Arabia among the amassed plans and models found.

We shared the camp with the Americans and with the use of their facilities life was quite comfortable. We still deployed forward to the border areas with Iraq but it was nothing more than a show of force. We conducted numerous exercises deep in the desert and all the leftover war stock of ammunition that we could not fire we destroyed. There were Iraqi tanks and weapons strewn everywhere. We clambered over them and took trophy photos, unaware of the depleted uranium threat that would emerge in later years. When we were back in camp we were taken down to Kuwait city and shown the horrors of what the population had endured under the Iraqis: the once beautiful city in ruins, the torture rooms and the football stadium used for public executions. It justified why we were here. The people wherever we went waved and thanked us. British and American flags flew everywhere. What a change fourteen years would make when we returned to the same area again.

While we were out there I was introduced to the world of pen pals; this was long before Internet dating and chat rooms. You would pick an address from the monthly *Soldier* magazine and write off in the hope of a reply. My best mate Chris and I would pick our prey randomly and give ourselves more and more outrageous stories to base our characters on. On one of our more crazy storylines we said we were American marines who had been attached to the British Army for the duration of the war. The two girls we wrote to were from Essex and fell for our story hook, line and sinker. We would say that we had just parachuted in from 18,000 feet and had taken out an Iraqi bunker system and while getting a brew on had decided to write our girls a letter. The two ladies in question took all of this in and would send us bags of toiletries and sweets and their undying love. This carried on for a couple of months before one of the guys who was receiving no mail decided to send a return letter stating that we were not Americans and the highest we had ever jumped was from the back of a four-ton truck. He also stated that if any more mail came to us he would send them a letter bomb through their postbox. It took us a few weeks to convince them the guy was a liar and we were just poor American country boys who had done nothing wrong but fall for some lovely English roses. The truth was these girls were fat gruesome double English cheeseburgers rather than pretty English roses. With our excuses believed we decided it was time to go in for the kill, and asked for their fat hands in marriage. They agreed! I know there are lonely people out there and I know what we did was probably wrong but, come on! To end this crazy interlude we then got one of the guys with really neat handwriting to send them both a letter saying we had been killed in an ambush while trying to defend a small village from pillaging and raping Iraqi soldiers. We were imaginary heroes who would be remembered by a couple of fat birds for years to come.

Just before we left the Gulf we were lucky to escape relatively unscathed from an American accident that could have been a lot worse than it was. As the Americans were checking through their ammunition stocks on the vehicle park in St George's Lines the intense heat set off some of the ammunition and the fire that ensued set off even more ammunition. Before long it was like a fireworks display but the rounds were shooting off all over the camp. Everyone ran for cover and for those who couldn't find an armoured vehicle, the next best place was over the perimeter wall. There were half a dozen injuries on our side, one serious with shrapnel wounds. The Americans lost two dead and quite a few seriously injured. Who needs an enemy when you live with the Yanks?

We spent four months in total in the Gulf before we returned to Germany and were then sent on leave. I flew to Spain and met up with the family with my tales of faraway places and lots of photos to back it all up. I was also in training for my upcoming Junior Non-Commissioned Officers Cadre, which started directly after leave. With my desert combats and Bergen (back pack) I would go tabbing through the hills around my parents' house and then spend the rest of the day digging and clearing weeds. They must have thought I had lost my head. I remember one day my dad wanted to spar with me. As I feigned a jab I came across over the top with a right hook and caught him. He backed away and couldn't believe he had been caught. I had a harder time believing I'd actually managed to not only hold my own but probably better my old man. Mum had been watching and stopped it straight away. Another time my old man came along on one of my runs and stopped me on one of the hills, out of breath, and asked me if I was in the SAS. He had seen lots of pictures of me wearing kit I'd bought myself which was obviously non-issue leading him to believe I was in a Special Forces unit. I finally convinced him I wasn't and that what I was doing was what everyone did to ready themselves for the cadres like this but it was still good to see the pride in his eyes. It was a good leave and it was great to spend time with my family again.

The JNCO cadre started in earnest straight away after leave, and the next seven weeks were the hardest I had ever done. We were up before first light every day and thrashed by the training staff till we felt as if our very souls were being ripped from our bodies. Trainer runs, Bergen tabs for hours and circuits in the gym followed by lessons and then deployments onto the training areas for infantry battle lessons. Every waking moment was spent learning and preparing to be an infantry leader of men in camp and out in the field. Seven weeks later I passed the cadre, went down town with my newly-purchased car, drank a lot with my mates, drove it home, crashed it, got caught by the German police, threatened the German police, and then proceeded to get my drunken head caved in by the German police. On my return to camp the Regimental Sergeant Major threatened to kill me and threw me in the nick. In twenty-four hours I had lost my chance to get made up for one year, got a one year ban from driving and lost £6,000 on my newly written off car, my insurance becoming void due to being drunk. I would continue paying for a car I didn't have for the next three years.

It was about this time that I received a call from my grandmother in Holland telling me that my dad, who was working out of Singapore, was in a serious way in hospital out there. Details were sketchy but it was classed as life and death. My Mum and sister, Michelle, had already flown out and I had to get there as soon as possible. I was a private soldier and as it was near the end of the month I was broke. I asked the army to fly me out but they would only get me as far as Heathrow, which was the opposite direction from where I needed to go. As a last resort, I phoned my dad's company and they said if I could get to Heathrow they would have a ticket waiting there for me. Four hours later I was at Heathrow waiting for my flight out to Singapore.

As I approached my dad's bed in the Singapore hospital I stopped in shock. The normally big man I had known all my life was a shell of his former self. He had been in a coma for a few days by now and already his body had withered. I put my hand around his forearm and felt nothing but coldness. The only thing keeping him alive was a set of machines. The story was he had woken up on the rig with a tingly numb sensation down his left side. As he was near the end of his month shift they had sent him for tests straight away. He had walked into the hospital himself and they had conducted a series of tests with dye being injected under his arm pit and an X-ray taken following the path of the dye as it moved through his brain, looking for any blockages. At some stage he had an allergic reaction to the dye, his body switched off and he had gone into a coma. Was someone to blame in the hospital? We will never know. The decision to turn off the life support machine was given and Dad passed away later that evening. He was a larger-than-life man and the doctors had said even if he had been able to breathe by himself again, he was technically dead. He would never walk, talk, remember anything and would control no body functions. He would be a shell. He would never have wanted to live on if he had known this is what his future life was to be. As I left the hospital with Mum that evening it was the most crushing, devastating and final moment of my life. For my dear mum, her entire universe had collapsed.

Hasty arrangements were made for the cremation and we all flew back to Spain, a shattered family, not knowing what the future held. Mum and Dad had the closest relationship I have ever known two people to have. After twenty-five years of marriage they were more in love with each other than when they had first met. As I grew up I would be embarrassed as they were always holding hands and kissing. Flowers and romantic meals were the normal score. I didn't realize how unique and special the relationship they had was until I was much older.

I flew back to Germany a couple of weeks later, leaving Mum to try and find out where she would now go without him in her life. I felt I was doing no good just sitting around the place, the tears would flow at the mere mention of his name and I knew the mourning period would go on for many, many more years to come. What did it mean to me? It meant I had lost a dad, a man I had looked up to all my life, a man I admired, loved and wanted to not just emulate but better one day. With his passing I contemplated things I should have said to him, should have done with him. With my hero now gone I had nothing to prove to anyone but myself, and for a while my life seemed to have little direction.

I decided at this time of my army career that I wanted to call it a day and try to get myself set up on the oil rigs like my dad. I put in my termination papers, which gave me my last twelve months service in the army. I had been moved to the Regimental Police in the camp and with this new job I gained more power. We were the RSM's boys and enforced his discipline in and around camp. There were five of us on the team and as we patrolled around the camp we would shout a lot and prance around like we owned the place, which wasn't far wrong. There was never a lack of people who had messed up around camp and had been put on staff parade each evening. These people would have to turn up in their number two dress uniforms and be inspected. This would be followed by a two hour work period doing cleaning and painting jobs around camp followed by a final parade in uniform at ten that night.

The RSM at the time was a bitter little man who used his powers to harass people and shout and scream as much as he could without actually meaning or saying anything of much sense. He had very little respect from anyone in the camp and his way of getting people to notice him was by messing everyone around with his bullshit. How he had the nerve to pick guys up for being untidy or not turned up to the right standard of dress when he was the scruffiest little bastard in the camp I do not know. He had such a bad stutter that when he used to shout at people you would have to put your waterproofs on to stop being covered in spittle.

While in this job there were six soldiers who been caught doing drugs and were waiting for their discharge from the army. Their room was next to mine and one night I caught them all smoking joints. As they were already being booted out I decided to harass them by saying if they didn't each pay me a hundred German marks I would inform the head shed and their get-out dates would be extended. A few paid, a few gave me their televisions in payment, and the final character refused everything so I took his car. The next day he went to the Medical Officer and said I knew he had a drugs problem and was taking advantage of it by stealing his car and bullying his mates. The Royal Military Police and the Special Investigation Branch came into camp the very next day. I was arrested and my room searched. Five television sets and a Nintendo game console were removed and every previous misdemeanour I had ever had was dragged up.

While in the job a few months previously a prisoner had done a runner from the guardroom and as I gave chase he had tripped over on the pavement outside camp and came up fighting. I was still in full flight when my right hook caught him full on the jaw. The last thing he saw before unconsciousness was his teeth sailing past his head. This had happened months ago and had been put aside, but it was now rearing its ugly head again. As well as that there was another incident where a prisoner had tried to get out of one of the cells and I had been forced to hit him. Again, this was now brought up. While on exercise last year in Canada a soldier from another unit had kicked me in the head while in a taxi. I had retaliated and put him in the hospital. I had done this in self defence and had been cleared of the incident. The picture they were trying to paint of me was not pretty. A few scraps downtown where I had been arrested for fighting with some Germans now rounded off their picture of me being a bully. My final few months in the army were filled with interviews and the threat of a two-year stretch for bullying, grievous bodily harm and theft. I may have not been an angel but I was none of the above. As it was, the investigation eventually fell by the wayside, with most of my so-called victims out of the Army and not interested in pursuing their initial complaints. As the charges were dropped I left the front gates of the camp for the final time with a bitter pill between my teeth.

I had completed six years service in the army and as I walked down the road towards Celle I didn't have a clue what I was going to do. I was just glad to be out of the army.

CHAPTER FIVE

May your soul already be in heaven an hour before the devil knows you're dead. - traditional Irish toast

FOR MY PRE-RELEASE COURSE I had returned to England and did a Fire Fighting and Rescue Course, which was compulsory before being allowed to work offshore in the North Sea. I had sent my CV off and was told that there was a minimum six-month waiting list before being considered for the oil rigs. This was way too long for somebody with no money coming in and no roof over his head, so I sacked that idea and started work with a German building firm as a labourer. With a job and income now sorted I moved into my sister's attic for six weeks while I looked for my own place. My sister, who had married a British soldier and moved to Germany a few months earlier, was paranoid about me being set loose in her house so she gave me the attic room, with its single light bulb and single bed. It was like a prison cell but more uncomfortable. Nevertheless, it was free and was a means to an end.

   I had no toilet in my room and had to go downstairs to use my sister's; if she was in that is. She would not trust me with a key. God, was I really that bad? One morning I came down for the call of nature and they had gone out. Panic! I had nowhere else to go so in desperation I ran into the back garden and with a shovel in hand dug a shallow grave for my needs. It was early and not fully light so imagine my surprise as halfway through the deed I looked up and saw the neighbour looking at me in horror as I was having a poo in the garden. There was nothing I could do at this stage except smile and wave cheerfully, saying, Good morning!

She obviously did not want a conversation with me and drew the curtain with a violent tug.

My sister was petrified when I told her the story and couldn't believe what I had done. How could she ever face her neighbour again? The final straw came when her husband's parents came to visit, they were a bit posh and I was under orders not to swear, get drunk or have a poo in the garden. As the BBQ was under way later that day I stumbled back in from a bit of a session downtown with some of the lads. I had on a cut-off Harley Davidson T-shirt, was covered in tattoos and was more than a little drunk. As I sat there at the BBQ I leaned back on the garden chair, swearing as it fell backwards. As it hit the ground I lay there giggling and then fell asleep. I think I had overstayed my welcome more than somewhat at my sister's. A few days later I moved out to an apartment a couple of miles outside of Celle.

My time out of the army and working on the German network was hard work to say the least. I was so set on leaving the army I had paid little interest as to where I would live once I left, where I would work and most importantly, how I would communicate with all my new-found German work colleagues. Just because we had won the war and they all should speak English as their first language because of this, didn't wash in reality. My German chat-up lines and how to order a beer didn't help in the least on a building site.

As I turned up for my first day at work with my packed lunch in hand I was surprised to see my work buddies, called Norbert and Zigfried, open up a can of beer before driving in the work van to our first call of the day. My first job was back in my old camp. I tried in vain to explain I shouldn't go back there but to no avail. As I dug down towards the burst water pipe below A Company's block the guys caught sight of me digging and the piss taking began. It wasn't long before people were throwing things at me and generally being a pain in the arse. It was a long day. The next day found us digging up pipes on some crappy road in the middle of nowhere with Ziggy and Norbert half pissed by midday. The ground was like concrete. I had been chipping away with a pick for over two hours and getting nowhere when Norbert opened up the van, took out a jack hammer and proceeded to churn up the ground in minutes. They were both in hysterics and I was on the verge of killing my first German.

As the winter months drew in and the weather dropped to zero the road crews would lay off half the work force and invite them to return in the spring. As I was the new boy I was the first to go. I quickly found more work with a floor-laying company and found myself away from Monday to Friday in what was the old East Germany. The place was a dump and the West Germans' joy at the wall coming down had now changed and they saw it as a curse as the country ploughed billions of marks into their rebuild. These were hard days with long hours of heavy labour but I enjoyed it as it kept me fit and as the weeks became months and the daily regime of working out in the cold hit me, I decided to move on again.

Between jobs I decided to take my current girlfriend over to Spain to visit my sister and her husband who had moved there after he had finished his stint with the army, the year before. It was going well until the fourth day there. We were all out clubbing and I asked my sister why she didn't go to see Mum very often. After all, she lived only half an hour away up the coast. My sister burst out crying and said it was because her husband beat her and she had black eyes and bruises and didn't want Mum to see her. I saw red and in a blind rage swung a haymaker that knocked him down to the ground. As I went in to finish him off my sister threw herself onto him to protect him, while my so-called girlfriend went to get security from a local hotel onto me. How the hell had this happened? Now I was the bad guy. The next day, when the beer had worn off, he had a battered face with black eyes to match, I had an ex-girlfriend and Mum thought I had filled him in because I had been pissed. Not wanting to rock the boat any more I returned to Germany feeling lower than a snake's belly.

Something that should be put in at this stage and was a big part of my life was my son, who had been born a couple of months previously. Just before my dad passed away I had met a German girl, Uta, and had an on-off relationship with her for about eighteen months before she told me she was pregnant. I don't care what anybody thinks about abortion, if you bring a baby into this world for the wrong reasons then which is the lesser of the two evils? She had told me she couldn't have children and then dropped the bombshell that she was pregnant. My life was far from stable and I found it hard enough to look after myself, let alone a little shit machine. I gave her the ultimatum, to have an abortion, or face the fact she would bring up a baby by herself. She chose to keep him. I carried on with my life by myself, which is the way I preferred it.

Meanwhile, back in Germany, my last job while I was a civilian was with an ex-soldier who had set himself up in Germany with a parcel delivery service. I started driving for him and had my own van and a mobile phone, which was part of a battery-pack suitcase and was a new thing. I felt like a high executive. I used to walk into the pub with my mobile phone suitcase, make a call and people actually thought I was cool. I think? I had signed a lease on a new flat in the centre of Celle and was enjoying the single life again. My German was getting better and I could hold a full conversation with the locals by now, and just when I thought things were as good as they could be, I blew the lot on one stupid night out. I went out for a few drinks and met an old girlfriend and decided to make a night of it. Later that night as we left a night club I decided that instead of waiting for a taxi I would drive us home myself. We mounted up in what may as well have been a space ship as I don't remember much about getting behind the wheel. About 500 metres down the road the traffic light was on red and two stationary cars were invisible to me until I smashed into the back of the first one and that in turn went into the back of the other one. I sobered up instantly, but what lay before me would not go away, and would shape my life thereafter.

My car was totally written off and so was the car I had run into. The first car in line had its back caved in but the driver was okay. The woman in the car I had hit seemed okay initially but later went to hospital with whiplash. When the police came I was breathalysed and arrested immediately. I was so drunk they couldn't believe I could walk, let alone drive. I would have to foot the bill for my car, the woman's car and the repair bill for the third car. I would have to pay the woman's medical bills and her wages for two weeks missed work. I lost my licence for two years and would have to take the test again, in German, as well as see a shrink. In Germany, they reckon you are mad if you get done more than once for drink driving. They may have a point. I lost my job, as it required driving, and with it went my beloved mobile phone suitcase. As I had no job I could not afford my flat. In the big scheme of things I was up shit creek with no paddle and a hole in my boat to round it off. The whole amount of money I owed was 60,000 Deutsch marks, which came to around £20,000. I deserved everything I got and was lucky I hadn't killed anyone, but by God I felt sorry for myself.

My guardian angel took the form of a company commander I had known from old. He had heard I was in a world of hurt and came to me with a Get Out of Jail Free card. He offered to get me back in the army straight away. I would go into his company and he would get me back to the UK as soon as possible. All I would have to do was box for the company and as soon as the boxing was finished go back to the UK and attend Junior Brecon on a Section Commanders Course. I was to leave everything as it was in my flat and leave a note saying I had gone to join the French Foreign Legion. All the red tape was forgotten and the next day I turned up in camp and started boxing training with A Company. Another ex-soldier and a very good friend of mine re-enlisted at the same time; again the same company commander orchestrated his return.

CHAPTER SIX

Dream what you want to dream; go where you want to go; be what you want to be, because you have only one life and one chance to do all the things you want to do. - author unknown

TWO YEARS OUT OF the army and being a lazy civilian had taken its toll on my body and the training hurt me like never before as we were brought up to fitness in the short amount of time left before the boxing began. I boxed at light heavyweight and cruised through the preliminary bouts to the final. The final saw me lose out to a big experienced black guy on points, but having had two years out I reckon I did okay.

The battalion was moving back to Warminster in the UK in a couple of months and I had started to see my baby boy, Cody, more and more since his birth a few months before. The guilt trip kept coming back to haunt me and I felt if I were to move back to the UK I would lose touch with him and regret it for the rest of my life. I made the decision I should marry and move my wife and son back with me in order to keep him in my life. Uta and I took the train back to the UK the following week and did a quick registry office job in Grimsby as we had friends there, returning to Germany as man and wife. Within a couple of months I knew I had made a big mistake.

When we arrived in Warminster we were housed in one of the smallest flats I had ever seen. My wife burst into tears, my lad was crying, but I thought it was better than living in the block in camp. Being a single soldier up until this point it was a culture shock having to share my living space with a whingeing wife and a smelly small person, and worst of all my money was always gone. We had only been there a short time and I was off on Junior Brecon up in Wales, about a two-hour drive away. I had thought my NCO's cadre had been hard and expected this to be worse but the myth that surrounds Brecon is just that, a myth. The course itself was huge, with over 200 students from all the infantry regiments turning up. We were told not to unpack our bags until we had completed the basic personal fitness test and then the Infantry Combat Fitness Test. The boxing had got my fitness back up to a good standard and I thought the fitness tests here were easy. There were a lot of people who hadn't found the fitness tests easy though and all those who failed were packed back onto buses and returned to their parent units, a harsh but necessary action. If you couldn't pass the basic tests there was no way you could cope with the demands the course would throw at you over the next couple of months, and to tell you the truth if you couldn't pass the basic tests you shouldn't have been sent here in the first place.

On a course like this it was best not to stand out too much, especially at the start. As we all packed the large main lecture hall on the first day's brief, the parachute captain who was giving us the first brief looked up at the rear of the lecture hall and lost his temper. "You, Cowpat head!" He was looking in the general direction where I was, so I looked behind me to see what the commotion was all about. Again he bellowed. "Yes, you, Cowpat head!" He was looking directly at me. I was told to make my way down to the front of the theatre where he ripped into me about my hair cut. I basically had a long tuft of hair on top and a zero back and sides; with a bit of gel applied it was awesome. At Brecon however it was considered unprofessional and I was ordered to have the rest of my hair shaved by that afternoon. So much for being the grey man.

The course itself was split into two, the first half being the tactics phase and the second half being the skill-at-arms phase. The tactics phase was six-weeks long and was a brutally hard introduction to life as a section commander in the field. We would do all of our fitness with a weighted Bergen and platoon weapon systems, and then after a quick rest be taken out to the training area and thrown into section attacks and battle lessons. The pace was relentless and as we moved out of the river beds crossing the line of departure for yet another attack I looked left and right of me at the cold, wet soldiers and felt a deep pride in being part of this. Nobody wanted to be here but through all the hardships everybody had come together and we were looking the part. I couldn't help but think that if this was for real it would take something extra special to stop us. As the first explosions started raining down with a mixture of high explosive and smoke rounds we waited for the last round to land before launching into our assault. You knew as you darted to the next piece of cover you would be covered by fire from the rest of the fire team and you in turn would lay down fire for the other guys to move. It was hard, demanding work and every Friday you would be shattered. After weapon inspections and final briefs we were released for the weekend with orders to report back late on Sunday for the start of the next weeks training. Most would just collapse onto their beds for a marathon sleep while the hard core would get their disco kit on and head into Brecon town centre for beer and the chance to score with some of the local chicks. I would jump onto the transport home to see the family, though I didn't really see a lot of them because as soon as I got home I went to bed and the rest of the time I spent getting my kit ready for Sunday.

After the tactics phase had been completed we were given a long weekend and then returned to Brecon to complete the skill-at-arms phase of the course. This was a pain in the arse, with many long hours spent with your head in a pamphlet preparing weapons lessons and battle lessons out in the field. Every night you would have a minimum of three lessons to prepare for the next day. It was impossible to get every lesson learnt to the same standard so as long as you knew the format for the lessons, which were all the same, you would play the numbers game and hoped you weren't called up. Most of the time you could safely say when the directing staff (DS) would call you up, but every now and then they would catch you out and as you stood in front of the class your brain would register zero and your grade would register a big fat Freddy. Six weeks later, I walked out of Dering Lines at the end of the course and was qualified as a full corporal. I would still have to wait a while before the regiment actually promoted me but the hard work had been done.

On my return from Brecon I was again put on the boxing squad and did the normal six-week build-up training. My fitness was at a high standard because of my time at Brecon and this time I boxed at heavyweight. The prelims went by smoothly and at the semi-finals I had a bye straight through to the final as the guy I was to fight had been injured in his previous bout. The big night came and I cruised to a points win over my opponent, finally taking a win in the final.

My mate, Stu, who had gotten back into the army at the same time as myself back in Germany, had just completed the SAS selection course. He was back in the battalion to turn in his kit and complete his documentation before moving up to Hereford and after a long chat with him I put my name down for the next summer's selection course. Before being put onto the course you had to complete a briefing weekend up at Hereford so with my dates confirmed off I went.

The joining instructions gave a time to report and it was a good job I arrived early as it was a nightmare to find the camp. On arrival it was the normal score of documentation, kit and room allocation. Over the next few days we were taken on gradually harder runs, briefs and then the military swim test with a high water entry that left my testicles near my throat. In the evenings I would go around to my mate's house and listen to his advice on the selection course and what routes I should run prior to attending. The final day of the briefing weekend saw us all do a Military Basic Fitness Test of a mile-and-a-half run in your best time followed immediately by a two-mile battle run and then just when you thought it couldn't get any worse an eight-mile Combat Fitness Test. By the time I headed home my body felt as if I had gone the distance with Mike Tyson. I was a moving mass of pain; but I had done it. It all sounded possible and I relished the day I started selection.

On my return to Warminster I made the decision to jack in my marriage, packed my bags and moved into the block yet again. I had about six weeks before the start of the course and needed to give my build-up training all my effort and concentration. I could not afford to go through all the hassle at home and give it my all on selection. The weakest link had to break, and that was my marriage. Six weeks later and I felt fitter and more focussed than I had ever been in my life.

As I drove up to Sennybridge camp in Wales, I was fighting a huge battle in my head. Part of me wanted to turn around and head home while the other part was saying that I was ready for this and everything would be alright. As I entered the camp and booked my car in I was told to head straight for the cookhouse and turn in my documentation.

The cookhouse was packed with soldiers from every regiment you could think of and then a few more. Lots of the guys that came to try their luck here came with other members from their units, they would have done all their training together and it was a source of comfort to have someone you knew with you when the going got tough. In my eyes it was also a hindrance as if your mate fell by the wayside it could have the domino effect with others following shortly afterwards. They used the 'Yes I failed, but I got further than him' attitude. I did my paperwork and was given the equipment I would need for the course and allocated a room, which I shared with about fifteen other guys. There was quietness to the room as everybody prepared their Bergens with the right weight and equipment for the Combat Fitness Test, which was to be carried out early the next morning. Preparation complete, I lay there in the darkness and listened to the nervous chatter of the guy's until I drifted off to sleep.

The next day was overcast, cold and drizzly, just like my mood. We lined up next to the Bedford trucks and had our names crossed off a master list, our Bergens checked and weighed, and then we mounted up on the trucks in readiness for the trip to the start point. Most of the guys looked focused and extremely fit; they were drinking energy drinks and generally looked the part. I was psyching myself out here. The only non-issued thing I had on was a pair of decent walking boots and as I reached for my issued water bottle I felt like a tramp, these guys must have spent a fortune on all their kit. It did look good though.

When your kit was weighed it had to be smack on or over but never under weight, if it was you were given a stone to carry which was signed by one of the DS. It would be checked at the end of the day. The stone would always be a monster and would take your weight for the day well above what it should have been so it was to your own benefit to ensure you had the correct weight to start with. The weight had to be usable weight and not stones and sand or they would dump it and weigh you again. They would also search you for mobile phones and Global Positioning Systems (GPS). If either of the last two were found on a person they would automatically be kicked off the course as this was classed as cheating. The course was split into groups for ease of control and then we were off. My mate who had passed the previous course had told me not to stay with the DS as they would push the pace quite hard, just sit somewhere around the middle. The aim was to be the grey man who did not stand out for being a show-off or an idiot.

The pace we set over the ground was not that fast or hard but the route was. If we were not running up what felt like sheer cliffs we were digging our heels in and shuffling down steep gradients, only to start the big climb back up again. It wasn't long before the group was spread out over a large area and doggedly I kept myself roughly in the middle, keeping the lead group just in sight. One hour and fifty minutes later we crossed the finish point at Kelly's Corner, a small hut on the training area. It had been a hard tab but I had finished and had more in me if needed. I was happy. A lot of people weren't happy that day though and as we got back to camp those who had not passed in the set time were turning their kit back in, collecting their documentation and heading back to their units, their dream finished.

The rest of the week went on like this, every morning up early, kit weighed, onto the trucks and then whatever march we had for that day. As the kit became heavier, the distances longer, the daily regime was taking its toll on my body. My feet were mummified with zinc oxide tape and my back padded against the rubbing of my Bergen. My whole body was one massive ache; the one thing that kept me going was the weekend off ahead and the people falling by the wayside, of which there were many now. At the end of the first week we came to the next big hurdle, the high walk. This consisted of a twenty-three kilometre tab in an undisclosed time going over the infamous Pen y Fan peak (the highest in

South Wales), twice in the process. This time I found it hard to keep the main group in sight and I was on my last legs as I crossed the finish point at the Storey Arms car park. When I first came in the DS told me to move off to the right and I thought I had failed, it wasn't till I got to the vehicle that I was told I had passed and we made our way back to camp, knackered but happy and looking forward to the fact that we had two rest days ahead of us to recuperate.

The second week was similar to the first with longer and heavier marches but this time individually done to test our navigational skills as well as our fitness and determination. When you are out in the hills with the weather and terrain closing in on you, the straps from your Bergen threatening to wrench your shoulders from their sockets and your feet on fire from friction burns your mind becomes your worst enemy, or your greatest ally. Before long you find you are talking to yourself and a list of reasons why it would be easier if you just stopped and gave in are forming in your head. It becomes a lonely place to be and mental stamina and positive thinking play as important a part as does physical robustness.

The third week started on a Sunday, with our goal to make it to Wednesday when Test Week began. Two days before Test Week, on one of the Lodestone marches held in the Black Mountains, I went over on my left ankle while trying to read my map and run at the same time along one of the many sheep trails. I undid my boot laces to compensate for my swelling ankle but by the third check point I had dropped behind so far the DS pulled me off due to safety reasons. I argued the point half-heartedly but I knew my dream was over. Later that night, I packed the last of my gear into my car and drove home with my torn ligaments in my ankle pounding. I was given the opportunity to return and try again on the next course but I knew that I would not take them up on the offer. You had to have your mind focused and to want this more than anything in your life and I knew I would not get this focused again.

On my return to camp I was greeted by a huge amount of piss taking which I had expected and I was also told that as soon as I could do physical activities again I was to join the boxing squad for the upcoming Inter-Companies event. That was the only thing with boxing within the army, once you got into it you couldn't easily get out. The weeks in track suit and the extra leave granted were also a big reason to do it. When the boxing came about I boxed heavyweight and got myself through to the finals, but this year I was stopped in the second round by a big right hook that had me seeing stars. As with amateur boxing, although I didn't go down, the referee could see I was hurt and stopped the bout. I was happy as I have no doubt that if I was left to box on I would have received a sound battering.

Married life for myself was not what I had expected. I had briefly moved back home during selection and so I made a decision after yet another argument to move into the block again. My wife was given three months to find other accommodation while I still paid the bills and I started living the single life again. I ended up staying in the block for about two months before I moved back into the flat again, but things were never good and over the next few weeks I received picture but no sound from her. They were asking in camp for volunteers to go across with our First Battalion to Northern Ireland and I put my name down for a six-month attachment. I didn't think my wife was too upset when I said I would be going away for a while.

Arrival in Belfast this time was a more controlled experience as I knew what to expect, and I was not the new guy. I was a lance corporal and had my own team. We were part of a 'Poacher' platoon within the First Battalion group. They sent us back to Fort Whiterock and it was as if time had stood still; everything was as I remembered. The patrol matrix meant that our half of the platoon would do the twelve-hour shift of days and the other half would do nights. I enjoyed being in command and the trust and loyalty that was formed within the guys in my team. I knew they would cover my back and not let me down and they knew I would lead by example, sticking by them and in return not let them down.

After a couple of weeks in Fort Whiterock we were tasked with moving down to Springfield Road RUC station, a little police station with an army section set off to one side. From here we would patrol along the notorious Falls Road and all of the Republican trouble spots around the area. The stupidity and indestructibility of youth was upon me and there weren't many patrols we went on where something didn't happen. The platoon commander must have cursed the day he laid eyes on us.

One of the guys originally put in the team was an idiot so I made it my aim to get rid of him. Just before leaving the camp I would swap over the positions of all the team so they would not always carry the same heavy equipment. The lead scout would carry the lightest bit of kit as he would have the important job of being the eyes and ears of the team and would have to react first to any incident. Just before we left camp I told him to hard target out of the camp and turn left, with a wink to the guys I indicated right. As he sprinted off up to the left we all went right and carried on running. About a hundred metres down the road we stopped and shouted at him to join us. When he finally caught up we told him he was an idiot as everyone knew we were going right, he tried to argue the point but was told to shut up. He would write to dating agencies and get hundreds of replies and we would nick the addresses and return mail saying he was some kind of psycho, it got to the stage where they went to the police about him and he was cautioned. On one of the other patrols he was carrying the heaviest kit and I initiated a false contact running for about one kilometre before stopping, as he came to a halt he tripped and as his head hit the ground his kit smacked into the back of his helmet just about knocking him unconscious. We burst out laughing, he went to cock his rifle saying he was going to kill us and I was left with little choice but to knock him out. Every patrol we did from then on I would remove the firing pin from his rifle; a week later he went and saw the padre and was taken out of the team.

We would give grief to anyone that deserved it on the streets, whether they were known terrorists or just local thugs. On one patrol we noticed a known vehicle but didn't recognize the person driving it so we pulled it over. The person inside started shouting and being abusive and as we asked him to step out of the vehicle he made his way to the front door of one of the houses on the street. He refused to acknowledge us so I instructed one of the lads to threaten him with arrest. He barged past and started swearing and being abusive once again so this time I told my guy to arrest him, as he grabbed hold of the man's arm he went to swing for him. I was directly behind him and instantly grabbed him in a gooseneck hold around his neck, forcing him to the ground. He screamed and struggled like a madman and it took all my strength to hold him down, at the same time calling for assistance on the radio from the remainder of the multiple. As with everything in Northern Ireland, within minutes the whole neighbourhood had emptied onto the streets and we now had a crowd of about fifty people giving us grief. This was rapidly turning into a nasty situation. With the village idiot still in my grasp we did a slow withdrawal down the street in the direction of Springfield Road RUC station with the rent-a-gang in hot pursuit.

As luck would have it a local RUC patrol vehicle had heard about the commotion and positioned themselves between us and the crowd, promising violence if they did not move back to their houses. After a background check later on at the station it was revealed that the arrested person we had brought in was a local thug and drug dealer who was wanted by the RUC. We got a "well done" and he got time in the nick.

Another patrol had one of my guys attacked on the Falls Road by some cider-drinking freak swinging like he was Mike Tyson. We chased the drunk until he tripped over the pavement, giving me time to grab him by his throat and pin him to a wall while trying to cuff his wrists. He fought like ten men and was soon joined by a few more of Northern Ireland's finest piss heads. Just when we thought it couldn't get any worse, the local Republican bar emptied its contents of angry lager louts onto the street. There were twelve of us and about a hundred of them and more joining by the minute. Screeching tyres and swinging batons from the RUC came just in time for us; these guys took no prisoners and laid into the crowd with no mercy. When they had finished there were some seriously hurt people strewn all over the road; we had been called back to camp to explain ourselves yet again. Oh well!

After a few weeks based at the Springfield Road station we started doing shifts daily from Fort Whiterock camp. On one shift we completed our handover to the oncoming multiple for the night shift and started our journey back for the night. We had gone a couple of hundred metres up the road from the station when from an alley off to our right we were at the receiving end of a Republican double Prig attack. A Prig is an improvised Rocket Propelled Grenade. The first rocket flew high and missed the front vehicle by inches slamming into a training academy building twenty metres away. There was a blinding flash of light followed by a huge explosion. We thought the first vehicle had been taken on by an Improvised Explosive Device (IED) and accelerated to get around the static vehicle and into depth to cut off the terrorists' escape route. As we came level with the first vehicle a second explosion hit our vehicle and threw us sideways across the road. We continued down the road for a further fifty metres before the engine gave a horrendous crunch and died. The high explosive warhead of the Prig had hit the right-hand side wheel of our Land Rover, ricocheted upwards and into the engine block where it had exploded. A couple of inches further back and it would have penetrated the driver's door and killed us outright. I debussed the troops and prepared to follow up on foot but the Royal Logistic Corp driver remained frozen behind the wheel. The street was a scene of chaos with civilians running away from the contact point, some covered in blood from the explosions. I closed the guys in around the vehicle and sent a contact report while asking for medical assistance for the driver and civilians; he was in a deep state of shock and would later be medically discharged from the army.

When the area was cordoned off the contact point was found with both Prigs left where they were fired. Through intelligence reports given later we found there were over twenty people involved in the incident, with oncoming traffic blocked to give them a clear field of fire. The run-back route was covered by a machine gun mounted in a roof skylight, waiting for any follow up. Good job the driver had frozen or we would have gone down the run-back route and been hit by the machine gun. There was a local pub where they had run to and burnt their clothing before jumping into a get-away car and quickly headed out of the city. We would all count ourselves lucky as this was a well-planned operation against us and it just went to prove the saying that they had to be lucky just once whereas we had to be lucky all the time.

The tour had many incidents, too many to list, but it was the last tour in Northern Ireland I would do before it calmed down from the bad old days. Obviously things would stay bad, but not to the extent it had been, and in fact still was while we were there. Over my career I would do four tours in Northern Ireland, three in Belfast and one in East Tyrone. It was also just before returning from Northern Ireland that I was promoted to full corporal. A nice way to round off a good tour.

After my post-tour leave things were still far from going well at home so I put my name down for as many courses as I could. Six months away from home spending twenty pounds a week and I had come home to being seriously in debt with the bank. She had handed me a gas bill stretching back over six months. When I questioned her as to why she hadn't paid the bill she answered that she thought it just came round twice a year. My reply of "what the hell is it with you Germans and gas", brought another bought of picture and no sound. My wife had spent all the money on doing up the flat and buying clothes. I knew my marriage was going nowhere but was too scared to finish it so I decided the next best course of action would be to go away all the time.

THE FIRST COURSE THAT came up was the Jungle Warfare Instructors Course held in Brunei. I had always wanted to do something in the jungle so it was a good opportunity to test myself in that environment. I flew from Heathrow to Singapore, Business Class on Singapore Airlines. The flight was fantastic; as everything was free on the flight I decided to see if I could single-handedly empty their stock of Jack Daniels. I had seventeen hours and six films to watch as I doggedly began my experiment. I was slightly intoxicated by the time I arrived in Singapore. From here it was a change to Brunei Airways where people prayed before they flew. Why? What the hell was wrong with the plane? By the time we arrived at the Training Team Brunei camp I had a pounding headache and was probably not far off going down with heat stroke through dehydration. Why had I drunk so much? Two snobby officers who had sat next to me and drank orange juice while reading jungle warfare pamphlets for the flight shook their heads in that patronizing way someone looks at a small child who has misbehaved. To hell with them, I'd enjoyed my flight.

Most of the course was spent in the trees (jungle) and I loved it. This was basic soldiering and was run by grown-ups who treated us like grown-ups. Once you were dropped into the jungle that was you; there were no tracks or roads and the whole place had that middle of nowhere feel to it. We practised jungle navigation using pacing and bearings until we could safely find our way around the place with ease. All the live firing was done at close range and the SAS instructors threw out the normal safety arcs until we were firing inches from each other as we did camp attack after camp attack. The camp Close Target Recce groups (CTR) would go in the day before and then as first light penetrated the jungle canopy the attack would begin. The GPMGs would fire in from their fire support positions, firing on pre-designated bearings. The undergrowth would be shredded as the thunderous fire power lay waste to the camp. The assaulting troops would be on their bellies crawling across the forming-up point and line of departure, camouflaged sweating faces grimacing with the strain of moving across the ground. As soon as the fire support stopped we would be up and moving in section and then fire team bounds towards the dug-in bunker positions and wooden attaps (primitive houses built mainly from palm leaves). Once the camp had been cleared the DS would call everyone into the centre of the camp and give us all a hot debrief. A quick water break would be given, appointment changes, followed by a new set of orders for the next scenario.

It was hard, hot, thirsty work but there was no bullshit and we all knew this was as realistic as our training could be. It was not for everyone and some people just couldn't handle the feeling of being claustrophobic in the jungle canopy. As long as you could cope with that and being soaked with sweat all day it was fine. As soon as it gets dark in the jungle all movement ceases and you find a place to lay up for the night and sleep. Once you stand down from evening stand-to you would get your hammock set up and get out of your wet kit. This would be put into a waterproof sack and you would get into your dry kit. By morning it would be back into your wet stuff which by now would stink of ammonia, it was not a pleasant task and after time even the mosquitoes and leeches wouldn't bite because of our smell.

Once the course was finished you would emerge from the canopy looking like some kind of escaped Vietnam prisoner of war. Everyone must have lost an average of two stone, your combats had virtually rotted on your body and you had a beard a Taliban mountain fighter would be proud of. As soon as the kit and equipment was cleaned and accounted for we would head down town for a massage, hair cut and a cut-throat shave followed by a milkshake, burger and chips. Then it was time to plan our R&R (rest and recuperation). We had the choice of Miri, in the Malaysian part of Sarawak, Borneo, or a small island called Labuan, half an hour's boat trip away.

At Miri, a few of us booked into the classiest hotel we could find, which was cheap as chips but very posh and headed straight for the pool bar. There we were, twenty-four hours out of the jungle and now floating in some crystal-clear pool with a cold jug of beer in our hands; surreal. The four days we stayed here were spent being very drunk, singing crap Karaoke, which the locals loved, and chilling by the pool. I was still married and although it wasn't a great marriage I refrained from sampling the local ladies, lots of the guys did though. Some even came back with stories of meeting what they thought was a good-looking woman but finding out later they had just been getting off with a lady boy, or a chick with a dick. Some of these weirdos looked very good indeed and you had to remind yourself it was a man that was looking at you with flickering eye lashes.

A report was written on everyone attending the course and as I received my verbal debrief from the CO of the training team I was told I had received an instructors recommendation and was encouraged to return as an instructor one day. I was also informed that one of the students on the Jungle Tracking Instructors course which started in a week had pulled out and there was a place available if I wanted it. I had been here for nearly eight weeks and wanted a break but I also knew that the opportunity to return later and do this course was slim. Knowing this, I accepted.

The course started much the same as the last and before I knew it I was hanging below a Huey helicopter and abseiling into the primary jungle canopy 200 feet below. Once we had broken through the tops of the trees and reached the darkened forest floor below we unclipped from our harnesses and spread out in all round defence. With our instructors watching our every move we broke down into our teams and picked up the sign left by the enemy soldiers. The sign left was normally small broken twigs or damaged leaf litter all telling their own story. With heavy Bergens and rifles tucked into the shoulder we moved as fast as tactically possible in pursuit of our unseen quarry. After seven days on the track we knew everything we needed to know about the enemy and pre-empting their intent we were picked up by helicopter and moved to a rendezvous with a Gurkha company-sized group in preparation for offensive action. That night the CTR group closed in on the enemy camp and reported the information needed to launch the assault the following morning.

As dawn enabled us to see the colour green we checked our blank firing attachments on our rifles and moved out of the stream bed which marked the line of departure for the attack. We had laid in the stream all night shivering. The fire support opened up and we went noisy. Most of the enemy soldiers still lay sleeping in their hammocks as we swept through their camp, a few managed to return fire but were quickly dealt with. The sound of our cut-offs further to the north opening fire indicated they had taken out a few runners that had managed to escape our initial assault. The DS stopped everyone and closed us in for debrief points. For once they were smiling, it must have gone well.

As the course finished we were given our reports and I was awarded an instructors recommendation again. I knew I had found my calling in the jungle. By this time, I had spent the best part of two and a half months in the jungle and as we started the end-of-course piss-up later that evening I should have realized I couldn't handle the booze. When I woke up in the morning the first thing I noticed was everyone in the twenty-man room was staring at me as if I was an alien. As my eyes started to focus I noticed I was laying naked on my bed with what appeared to be vomit over my chest and as I looked lower I noticed my jeans and top were nowhere to be seen. I was then informed by my disgusted roommates that after leaving the bar the night before I had made my way back to the toilet where I had tried in vain to undo my belt. With no success there I had shat and pissed myself before dragging myself back to my bed and being sick. I spent the remainder of the day rehydrating myself and cleaning up my mess. I could never remember feeling so bad.

This time for my R&R I decided to try Labuan, and would not regret my decision. The place was an offshore banking island and had all the trappings you would expect. Top class hotels that were cheap to stay in and big shopping malls. It also had amazing night life.

We had a few drinks in the hotel to start off the evening and then headed down town. The first bar we went in we had only just got to the bar to order the first round of drinks when the 'mamasan' who was in charge of the girls came over and started haranguing us for money. She lined up all her girls and asked which one we would like for the evening. They were all nice. There were Filipino, Thai and Malay girls as well as every other part of Asia you could imagine, all holding the same one quality; they were gorgeous. For an amount equal to £25 you could have a girlfriend for twenty-four hours, the one stipulation was she had to be back for work the next evening. Then and there I decided to go against my previous decision to stay faithful and reached for my wallet. What the hell; my marriage was down the pan anyway. With my Filipino girlfriend in tow, I went clubbing. The next day I sauntered down to the pool with my new girlfriend and there before me were about a dozen of the guys also with their trophies alongside them. What a country; if I ever won the lottery this was the place to retire to.

CHAPTER SEVEN

He will show his goodness in the kindly consideration he shows those less favored than himself. It is the way one treats his inferiors more than the way he treats his equals which reveals one's real character. - Rev. Charles Bayard Miliken

THE BATTALION WAS COMING to its final few weeks in Warminster and was getting ready to move to Cyprus. Just before they left I was put onto the Light Role Recce Commanders course, which was held in Warminster. I decided it would be best to move the family over to Cyprus early and then I would return to complete the course on the completion of which I would be entitled to promotion to sergeant. The course itself was headed up by a complete arse of a guy from the SAS, which was unusual as most of the guys I had worked with from there were sorted.

The course was seven weeks long and again most of it was spent in the field. We would deploy out with Bergens that required two men to put it on your back due to the weight and once you were up and walking you couldn't go to ground and get back up unaided. You would move to your briefed areas and start digging, the course was mainly about digging observation posts behind enemy lines, and we dug at every opportunity. The idiot in charge would criticize every one of us for the smallest of things, and it didn't take long before I bit. After I gave one set of orders to the guys for over an hour covering actions on most things I thought could go wrong he stood up and ripped into me. During my orders I hadn't mentioned how I would extract the helicopter pilot from the burning wreckage of the helicopter if we crashed and when I synchronized watches with everyone there it wasn't the same as his. I pointed out to him that I also hadn't mentioned what I would do if the Earth was suddenly invaded by aliens and maybe his watch was on the wrong time, not mine. He lost the plot and threatened to have me beaten up by his SAS buddies and then kicked off the course. Very professional.

The end result was as I walked into the CO (Training Wings) office at the end of the course and he gave me a stand up fail, saying I was a shit soldier with a shit attitude. I was gutted and left a broken man. I knew I should have kept my thoughts to myself but to fail me on a few run-ins was outrageous. I went straight back to the battalion and put my name down for the very next course. This one I passed with flying colours and kept my mouth shut the entire time. My wish being, that one day in the early hours I would meet the prick that ran the course on some deserted railway somewhere and I could show him what I really thought of him.

I flew to Cyprus a few days later and got settled into army life in the Mediterranean. We had a large but simple house with a large garden and I even managed to get myself a car and two motor cycles, one a 125cc scrambler and the other a big 1400cc Suzuki Intruder, a beast of a bike.

The battalion would have to go to Jordan twice while it had its two-year tour in Cyprus, the first was a company-size exercise and the second was a battalion-sized six-week exercise. I missed the company exercise due to boxing but I was part of Recce Platoon for the battalion exercise. As we arrived in Jordan the first thing that came to mind was: What a shit hole it was. Poverty was everywhere. We were transported from the airport to the desert-tented training camp by coach, an unforgettable, uncomfortable three-hour trip. The roads were for the most part pot-holed dirt tracks broken by small hamlets of habitation.

When we finally reached our destination the training programme clipped in straight away with fitness and ranges taking up most of the first few days. We had a company of Jordanian soldiers attached to us for the duration of the exercise and their standard left us all wondering whether we would survive the live firing part of the exercise. Who needed enemies when you had dangerous, ill-disciplined friends like these?

The training was progressive and started from individual skills and moved up to section and company live firing exercises, culminating in a massive battalion live firing advance to contact and finishing off with a deliberate attack on an enemy re-enforced desert fortress. On one of the live firing ranges we did, the sentries informed me they had found what appeared to be a graveyard. If one of the Bedouins that wandered the desert died they would bury him where he fell and we had come across numerous grave sites since our arrival. I had read somewhere that in the old days these people would bury their dead with all their prize possessions such as gold and jewellery and the like. This was apparently to assist them in their afterlife. I may have misinterpreted this fact, and it may have been some other country or race of people, but as far as I was convinced on that day I was looking at the grave of an ancient king who would be covered from head to toe in ancient gold and diamonds.

As we removed the large stone that was positioned as the improvised headstone there appeared to be a small crypt beneath it. Laid there was the distinctive shape of a human body wrapped in a Hessian-type material. When the material was pulled away the skeletal rib cage and back bones of the long-dead Bedouin was clearly identifiable. As we searched the rest of the body for any sign of valuables it became obvious there were nothing to be had; this poor bugger was just that - poor. He would have to hope to meet some of his camels in the afterlife to pay his way there, or hope to have a rich dead relative willing to share. It was then that the thought hit me: his skull. How cool would it be to have a real skull, get it mounted in a wooden box with a bit of a light display and place it in the living room. Whoever he or she had been previously they had been a bit of a minger and must have had a bad hair day when they passed away as the bits that were still attached to the scalp were very dry and tatty and I won't even talk about the remainder of the blackened teeth. He or she was definitely in need of a good hair conditioner and a visit to Mr Colgate.

As one of the officers approached I quickly hid my new-found friend, Ed the head, and repositioned the slabs of stone over the crypt. I packed him away in a black bin bag and waited for the sea freight to be packed. Ed was about to go on an amazing holiday to Cyprus where I intended to introduce him to his new-found family. It took seven thick bin bags taped around him to stop the smell of the decomposing flesh.

After the gruelling six weeks running around the deserts of Jordan we were given a small R&R period in a place called Akaba, in Jordan, next to the Red Sea. Lots of the guys hit the beaches or went scuba diving while most of us in Recce Platoon just booked into the hotel and went hunting for the nearest bar. Even in a Muslim country like this there were still places to find alcohol and even women if you really wanted. We found our bar and continued on our quest for absolute intoxication.

With hangovers in tow we spent the next day checking out the local shops where I seemed to gain the attention of a few of the locals who wanted to arm wrestle me. I refused to get dragged into their games until half way through the day when I thought, what the hell. To take away the constant nagging of one shop owner I arm wrestled and beat him and then made my way back to the bar for a triumphant beer. No sooner had we all sat down for our beers when a group of locals dressed in their sheets and headdress came around the corner and spotted us. Thinking I had upset their culture by beating the shop keeper earlier on in the day I was sure he had rounded up all his mates and come for some pay back. As it was, many loud chants and hand waving towards us brought home the fact that he had brought his big mate from the gas works to challenge me for the title of arm wrestling champion of Akaba. He was big and hairy and smelt like Ed the head but he had the strength of a small child and I easily beat him. He duly disappeared and returned a short time later with another fat lump that I again beat, hoping this would be the last before I got too drunk.

My mate, who was quite pissed by this time, suddenly stood up and declared himself my manager and that I would now no longer arm wrestle but I would fight the hardest man in Akaba to the death. Everyone burst out laughing except me and the Jordanians. These people carried swords and guns and stuff and would probably quite like the idea of my head on their mantelpiece. As it was we had nothing to be worried about as there was a group of Jordanian plain-clothed policemen who had seen the whole incident and ushered the now riled-up locals away from the bar, leaving us to carry on getting drunk.

Two weeks after returning to Cyprus I received a phone call saying the sea freight had arrived so I made my way to the camp to pick up Ed. I had warned off my wife and told my son he had a brother called Ed the head with no arms and no legs. In hindsight I realize it was a pretty weird thing to do but at the time it seemed normal. Anyway, I made a concoction of cleaning mixtures in a bucket and left Ed to soak for the night. The following morning with the family gathered round we pulled out a very clean and white Ed with the best looking set of teeth to ever decorate a Jordanian Bedouin's mouth and a gleamingly white skull devoid of all hair. Maybe I would invest in a nice wig for my mate Ed.

The whole idea of setting Ed up in a wooden display box and lights never really seemed to happen. As my marriage moved further down the drain my wife blamed it all on us being cursed by Ed which I found very unfair on Ed and one day when I returned home from work he was gone. She had put Ed in the bin and he was now a part of some landfill site, one day no doubt to be part of a missing person or murder investigation when somebody finds a gleaming white skull with amazing teeth in among the rubbish.

It was time for boxing again, and after being strong-armed into boxing for the company once more I found myself cruising to two easy wins during the preliminary bouts and reaching the heavyweight final more confident than ever before. I had hit the gym really hard for the past year and felt bigger and stronger than I had ever felt before. I made the long walk to the outside ring on the hot humid night of the finals and didn't feel the fear and nerves that normally kept me company at this stage, instead I felt invincible. Good or bad, I climbed through the ropes into the ring and stared at my opponent. He dropped eye contact and then and there I knew I had won. As the final bell went I stood triumphant and no sooner had I got back to the changing room than a crate of beer was put in front of me. Here we go again!

After a couple of weeks leave for the boxing I was told to report to the Quarter Master where I was told I would now be part of the battalion boxing team. I had never been that bothered about doing the company boxing as it was only for a few weeks a year but the step up to battalion boxing would mean full-time training. I did not join the army to live in a track suit and get punch drunk, but my argument was not strong enough and the next day I reported for training. We had five weeks training before the battalion fought and in the Mediterranean sun our training began in earnest. It was in the fourth week of training that during a hard sparring session I came in with a big right hook and my opponent ducked down. My fist missed his head and my body connected with his and stopped dead, my shoulder carried on moving forward taking my shoulder socket straight out. The pain that coursed through my body was the worst I had ever felt and all I could do was to support my arm and threaten to kill anyone who touched me. I was driven the short distance to the medical centre where the on-call doctor was called in. When he walked in an hour later the Pakistani doctor, who could not speak much English, said he could not give me any pain killers as they may have to operate when they took me to the main hospital located on the other side of the island.

After a bumpy ride in the ambulance I arrived at the British hospital four hours after the initial dislocation. The pain was as strong as it had been from when my shoulder had popped out and as I was met by a Gurkha doctor at the Accident and Emergency my heart sank. Thankfully this doctor knew what he was on and administered morphine straight away. After a series of X–rays and nothing was found to be broken he wrapped my arm in a towel and pulled my socket out and with a squelch it moved back into position. The relief was instantaneous and after he slung my arm I was on the return journey home with a sick chit saying I could not box or play rugby for at least three months. That was my short stint in the battalion team finished and I would not box again for the rest of my army career. The next game of rugby I played a few months later and my shoulder popped again. The medic in attendance popped it back in straight away this time but the doctor told me if it went again I might end up with serious problems in the future.

It was not long after this when I realized for the final time that my marriage was a farce and decided to end it for good. I planned my extraction from the house like a military operation and as each stage was complete I would tick it off my list. When it came to the final day I waited until my wife had gone on her driving lesson and packed the car with the last of my stuff. Five minutes before she was due to return I put my son to bed and drove into camp, waiting for the phone call from the families' officer wanting my explanation. As it was I was given a slap on the wrist for just doing a runner and my wife was told she would have to leave the house as soon as possible.

Within three weeks she was on a plane back to the UK with my son and I was free. It would still take me a further six years to get my divorce through as she dragged me over the coals. It would end up costing me thousands of pounds in solicitor's fees before I was rid of her and even then monthly payments and a lump sum loomed.

A few months later and the battalion moved back to the UK to Chepstow, on the Welsh-English border. My money was still tied up in paying for all my debt in Cyprus. I thought I had covered all bases when I had moved out of the house but I had forgotten my cheque book and my wife had gone anger-shopping with a vengeance. In return I had a few long months ahead of me paying for that trip. As it was I also had to pay the bills in Warminster, where she had moved to, so to say I was broke was an understatement.

When the battalion moved back to the UK they gave everyone four weeks leave. For me, leave with no cash left me no choice but to look for extra work down town. I went straight to the local industrial site in the area and started work at a supermarket distribution centre, offloading and loading the constant line of heavy goods vehicles that came in and out twenty-four hours a day. The work was hard and the hours long. I lasted four days before some zitty-faced kid came in during one of my breaks and handed me a brush, ordering me to sweep up one of the loading bays. My first instinct was to hit him but instead told him to piss off. He looked at me in total shock before storming off towards the duty shift supervisor. Within half an hour I was called to the supervisor for a bollocking. I stood before the fat supervisor and before he could say anything I told him to shove his job up his arse and stormed out. My stint in Civvie Street was over. The remainder of my time on leave was spent living like a pauper in camp.

After the extra-long stint of leave I was asked if I would like to go away for six months to Belize as a Jungle Warfare Instructor on the training team set up at Airport Camp, half an hour outside Belize City. I jumped at the chance and would never regret it. The British Army did its entire individual instructional training for jungle operations in Brunei and then shifted the larger unit training to Belize where a small team of trainers gave direction to the courses.

Our boss was a warrant officer from the Small Arms School Corp (SASC), added to this team was a sergeant and two corporals. We would deploy to the jungle with a handful of locally-employed civilians and set up training camps and ranges in preparation for the units coming across. Unlike Brunei all the training areas in Belize were accessible by vehicles. It was a four-hour trip from Airport Camp to the main areas we trained in but the reality was wherever we wanted to set up we could, the entire country was a training area. When the units arrived we would meet up with their head shed and training NCOs and tailor the training packages to each individual unit's needs and objectives. On a typical package we would spend around three to four weeks in the trees and then after a few days rest in camp re-deploy back out for the final exercise.

I was given a set of lesson plans that I would deliver for each of the training packages and after the first few times they became second nature. Luckily enough for me, I had some of the best and most interesting lessons to give and as I added to the content I would have an enthralled audience sitting before me. I loved this job and as far as I was concerned I would have spent the remainder of my army career teaching out there.

Belize itself is one of the most beautiful countries I have ever been to, from its chilled culture to its vast rain forests and crystal clear Caribbean coast line and sandy cays. The time we had off while out there was never boring and the guys and I would book ourselves on the camp weekend speedboat trips to all the outlying cays and islands, which resembled something out of a Sandals 5-star holiday brochure. Everything was dirt cheap and we got reduced rates wherever we went as British Forces; we were living the dream.

Just outside of camp was a strip club called Raul's Rose Garden, which is famous in the military fraternity. This old rickety wooden building held a large selection of Central American beauties who danced and whored for your money. You could go for a drink or a meal and watch the dancers and if the mood took you have a night of passion; all for the pricey sum of ten or fifteen quid. Muslims had to strap bombs to their bodies to go to places like this; we just had to walk ten minutes out of camp - although these girls weren't any virgins.

We became regulars at the place and when the girls had time off they would ring us up at the camp and ask if we would like to take them out for the weekend. If we were free, and they were the nice ones, we would book them on the local boat with us and take them for a weekend on the cays. It cost us next to nothing for the hotels and boats and we would have stunning Latina chicks on our arms for a couple of days. They wouldn't charge us for their company, what they got in return was living for a few days in top hotels, eating and drinking - and being treated - well. What we got were sexy women hanging on our arms like girlfriends - and sex. We would walk down the beach with cut-off shorts and a can of beer in hand with our dolled-up-to-the-eyeballs girlfriends in tow and watch the glares from the American tourists. It was obvious to all who these girls were but we didn't care. They were the ones who had to go back to their hotel rooms and wake up in the morning next to their beached whales of girlfriends and wives. I on the other hand would wake up next to Miss Caribbean.

After a few months in Belize I put in for an extension to my posting order and received an extra seven months on the training team. I was also asked if I would like to fly to Brunei and be a guest instructor on the next Tracking Instructors Course that was being run there. With my final goal to be part of the Training Team out in Brunei I jumped at the chance to get my foot in the door out there. With a flight on business class nearly around the world I arrived again at Brunei Airport drunk. Would I never learn? My boss from Belize was also with me but he was a student on the course while I was an instructor; this would be fun, I could tell.

Being on the directing staff side of the course was an eye opener. As a student everything had always seemed so together and professional, what you didn't see was the whingeing and back stabbing that went on even here. As it was I was there to give one of the permanent instructors some time off which was fine by me. There was one other guy there as a guest instructor and we were told to go on some R&R and return in a week. Never being one to argue the point the other guy and myself jumped on the next available transport for the port and the fantastic place that was Labuan.

On my return to Brunei and the course I was told that I would lead an eight-man Gurkha patrol and lay a track for the students to follow. For anyone who has never worked with the Gurkhas they are talked about as if they are some kind of elite force. I can assure you, and anyone who has ever worked with them would back me up, this is as far from the truth as you can get. In all the time I have spent in the jungle they have always been the ones to go down with heat exhaustion and not been able to carry the kit required. They cannot map read to save their lives and as they are so communal their tactics leave a lot to be desired. As I met the section commander I told him it was his section and I was there to navigate and give direction to the various incidents that needed to be set up. I had gone about 500 metres when I stopped and asked the section commander where he thought he was. He smiled at me and asked where I thought I was. After grabbing him by his shirt front and threatening him he pointed at a spot on the map miles away from where we were. He didn't have a clue. I spent the rest of the course leading the patrol and every night we lay up I would sit alone and cook my boil in the bag while Johnny Gurkha and his buddies would get in a huddle, cooking and chattering until the wee early hours. It was a long and lonely time and I might as well have been on my own.

At the end of the course the other guest instructor and I were told we had another week before we were due to head back, so off to Labuan we headed yet again. My return flight to Belize was another alcohol-fuelled experience with a stopover at Miami to round off a good few weeks away.

On my return to Belize there was a big fancy dress party and piss-up organized at the NAAFI bar in camp and the guys and myself decided to get some Crusader Knights outfits made up at a local tailor. We had white sheets with large red crosses and wooden swords with mesh helmets and we looked the business. As the night got under way we proceeded to imitate Oliver Reed and become drunken bums with the decision made to visit Raul's Rose Garden to show off our costumes to the dancers. The walk down to Raul's was made all that more difficult by our Crusader dress pulling around our ankles, how women do it I will never know. It wasn't long into the walk that I noticed we were being followed by some black guys in an old Cadillac. Whenever we stopped they would shout how they were going to shoot us "white boys", and then reverse away at speed. This went on for a while until we turned together and with our wooden swords flailing wildly above our heads and screaming, "Freedom", and other Braveheart crap, stormed the vehicle. The shocked locals couldn't get their car into reverse quick enough and as we drew level the passenger, a big afro-wearing Caribbean guy got out confronting us. I was all over him like a collapsed tent and almost simultaneously my mate put an empty beer bottle through the back window of the car. The locals must have thought we were madmen and gathering themselves together sped off with promises of a violent return.

Later that evening as we all sat there watching the dancers and drinking beer through our mesh helmets the local police force arrived with the idiots from the car. I was pointed out straight away and asked to move outside. My mates who were dressed the same were left alone. In the car park the coppers told me if I produced a thousand US dollars for the broken window I would be allowed to go but if not then I would be placed under arrest. By this time there was a large group of locals gathered around me and the Cadillac driver was gobbing off. It was then that I realized I probably looked more like something out of the Ku Klux Klan rather than a crusader and was probably in a bit of trouble.

I asked for the military police to be called as it was my right and was duly informed I had no rights in this country. I in return informed the little copper that if it had not been for the British then they wouldn't even have a country called Belize and would be part of the greater Guatemala. This was not a good thing to say and as the little copper started to draw his truncheon I lifted my mighty wooden sword above my head and laughed the mad laugh of a condemned man about to die, burping in the process. Just as I thought I would be hung by the crowd the duty officer from the camp turned into the car park, and I have no doubt he saved me from having my wooden sword shoved up my arse.

I was taken back to camp with orders to explain myself to the RSM and commanding officer the next day. The RSM and CO, thank God, were understanding of the whole incident and realized I was not the one who had broken the window. They also realized that the police force was corrupt and if they got away with getting money off me they might take advantage of other soldiers based out here. They had a local solicitor take on my case, paid for by the army, and before I knew it I had my first court appearance in downtown Belize City.

I turned up suited and booted for my court case and the whole scene was something reminiscent of an old cowboy film set. The whole building, including the courtroom, was made of four-by-four wooden planks and the black judge sat looking down on all in his courtroom as if he were some chieftain observing his tribe. Everyone, including my solicitor, was dressed in jeans and T-shirts with sandals to finish off the formal attire. The poor little white boy that was me was left sweating in my new polyester suit like a paedophile in a school playground. Before I was given entrance to the courtroom they told me I would have to be handcuffed and kept in the holding cell until called for. The so-called holding cell was full of big sweaty black guys who were being held for murder and rape as well as drugs offences and when they saw me they began chanting "I want the white boy" and other such remarks. It took a while until I had it cleared that I would not have to enter the holding cell; after all I was here for a broken window for Gods sake, not the murder and pillage of a community of nuns!

What was to ensue over the next four months was a series of court appearances with me on public display and being referred to as the "white boy"; never once did they use my real name. My key character witnesses, the orderly officer and the RSM, both screwed up their statements, the orderly officer by stuttering like a machine gun and the RSM by giving the wrong date of the incident. This left me believing I was going to be found guilty, thrown in a local jail and be used as a bitch to one of the many 'Mr T' lookalikes that were in the holding cell.

The local jail was called Hattieville Prison and early on in the posting a few of us had the opportunity to visit this lovely institute. It was like something from the American chain gang films. Our armed escort had taken us around the prison to jeers and comments from the black and Latino population and shown us the one white prisoner being held there. He had been an ex-parachute regiment soldier who had been done for drugs and given a three-year stretch. When we saw him he was hunched over in the corner of his cell rocking back and forward with a distant crazed look in his eyes. He had been raped and beaten so many times his mind was destroyed and his arse probably resembled the Channel Tunnel.

With the prospect of being his cell mate I nearly cried with joy when the farce of a case was thrown out four months from when it had started. The mother of all piss-ups was set up that night and as I left the courtroom for the last time my triumphant smile said it all as I gave the Cadillac driver and his solicitor the middle finger.

Before I had left the UK on my Belize posting I had a couple of romantic weekends with one of the local barmaids. Her name was Sue and the guys nicknamed her 'Sue Dead', with the reasoning behind the name being she was old enough to be dead. She was only forty-two but to us that was old enough to have witnessed the last dinosaur join his mates on the extinct list. I had not left an address so when I received a letter to me with 'third tree from the right' on the envelope I thought, what the hell, and replied. I thought nothing more of it until I received a phone call from the Belizean Defence Force guard commander at the front gate saying there was a woman asking for me. I thought one of the dancers from Raul's Rose Garden had come to see me so I nearly choked when I got to the guardroom and saw this skinny English slapper with a large suitcase waiting for me.

They say time makes the heart grow fonder; well I reckon time makes your memory lie to you. As she stood there all white and skinny with one leg wrapped in a tuba grip bandage and pink high heels I can honestly say I thought about asking the guards to shoot her. She informed me she had come to visit me for three weeks and had sold most of the stuff in her flat to afford the ticket to get here. My first action had to be to get her out of sight and luckily enough I had my boss's house for a couple of weeks while he was away. Later on that night, I contemplated ways I could get rid of her. She came out of the shower with her housecoat on telling me that her feelings for me were strong and she wanted that I should see her as she really was. She dropped her housecoat and stood there completely naked and the tuba grip bandage removed from her leg. Years earlier she had been caught up in a car accident and her leg had been badly burned; it resembled a piece of burnt roast beef. I thanked her for the gesture but insisted she get dressed and cover her leg up again.

The next evening I made my plan to go to Raul's Rose Garden with the lads and informed Sue Dead that she was to lock the door of the house and stay inside as killer attack-dogs patrolled the camp grounds at night. She wasn't the brightest spark and believed everything I told her. To see how far I could push the story I then said we had to deploy to the jungle as the Army Air Corps was were conducting night flights and if anything happened we had to reach them before the Guatemalans did. I told her it was dangerous work and not to wait up, if I was still alive by the morning I would see her then. The next night I pushed my luck once more and took her to the NAAFI bar where I told her to wait for me while I dropped a mate off down town. Instead I went back to Raul's, returning about three hours later. She was furious with me and after I calmed her down she stormed off to the toilets and returned with a clump of toilet paper which she indicated I should wipe away some lipstick off my neck. As I laughed and told her it was obviously from her she went mad and said she didn't have that colour. It took me half an hour to convince her that the heat of Belize sometimes reacted with lipstick and slightly changed the colours. Luckily she was as thick as she was old so she believed me.

As it was I put together a plan to get rid of her a couple of days later with promises I would return to the UK a few days after her. I ended up shoving her in between chicken crates on some local bus heading for Cancun, Mexico, and with a cheerful smile from me and a frightened wave from her she was off. With the nightmare of 'Sue Dead' gone it was back to Raul's for an afternoon drink.

Our next training package which was due in was from my battalion and with them they brought an SAS guy to act as Chief Instructor for their package, with me being his 2 I/C. We deployed to the training area and set up all the training camps and teaching areas and put the guys through their paces, with some awesome live firing ranges and realistic dry training to wrap up a very good package. We built an improvised gym and every morning I would run my legs off trying to keep up with this lunatic from Hereford, taking my revenge with the weights later in the day. Any time off and we would head into the local villages for a few beers and I would watch as he would introduce himself as SAS to anyone that would listen. His take on it was if it helped pull the ladies then use it. I on the other hand had a hard time sexing up 2 Royal Anglian; it sounded like some religious cult. I lost count the amount of times I had to tell people it was the Anglians, not the Anglicans.

As we finished the first six-week package I was offered the chance to move out to the small adventure training cay just off the coast of Belize City for six weeks as a windsurfing instructor. Now I was about as much of a windsurfing instructor as I was a priest but a few weeks earlier I had visited the cay and been told by the chief instructor out there that as there was no windsurfing instructor on the island so I could not take out a board. I had lied and said I was an instructor and he had then passed on to other people that I had the Level One instructor qualification. This bit of information had then reached the commander of the incoming company from my unit and as they had a lack of qualified adventure instructors I was offered the six-week slot.

At first I had gone along with it as I had thought they were trying to catch me out but as I was making my way to the cay with all my sports kit I knew I was in a dilemma. Did I admit I had been lying or just go along with it? The way I saw it was so long as nobody died or was injured then I should be okay. When I got to the cay I buried my head in the latest Yachting Association publications on what is expected of a basic windsurfing course and set about getting my sea legs back with some crash windsurfing.

The small cay was situated in crystal clear waters teeming with an abundance of brightly-coloured fish. Out in the distance you could make out the breakwater of the waves crashing against the barrier reef that skirted the coast of Belize and as you approached the cay you would be awestruck by the fine white-sanded beaches and deep embedded lush green mangrove swamps off to the north. As I stood there on my board I couldn't believe my luck for being sent here. It was then I noticed about fifty metres away a dark shadow lurking just under the water with a fin breaking the surface. My mind raced back to my childhood and I immediately thought worst case scenario; man-eating shark. As it got closer my relief at seeing it was a dolphin was short lived as I realized how big the bloody thing was, it must have been eight feet long and it appeared to have big teeth and an amused look in its eyes. My thoughts then turned to what if it was a pissed-off aggressive dolphin? I needn't have worried as it playfully gathered speed past me and disappeared out of sight to deeper turquoise waters.

The daily programme would be to meet the incoming guys and brief them on the various activities followed by the military swim test. This would entail a 100 metre swim from the jetty out to a moored buoy and then back again. I would inform the guys that if they heard an air horn they were to make their way at best possible speed back to the safety of the jetty as there was a shark in the water. There was no danger of sharks around here but it was worth the look of shock and fear in everyone's face when they heard this. This was again nothing compared to the mayhem when for a laugh I would wait until everyone was out to the turn around point and sound the air horn. There would be about thirty people in a blind panic trying to get back with every stroke imaginable and it was a sight to behold. As people dragged themselves up on the jetty exhausted I would be on my knees with laughter, how I never got lynched as they realized it was all a joke I will never know.

Thereafter we would get the guys up and split them into the various activities which were sailing, windsurfing and scuba diving. Those people that were with me for windsurfing would split their time between surfing, volley ball and sunbathing and every night we would party. The local bar would boat out local dancers for the new platoons as they arrived and the whole cay took on a holiday feel. One of the girls that came out was a stunner so I waded in with my made-up story of me being the boss of the British Army and being posted here for two years; she fell hook, line and sinker for it. From then on I had myself a girlfriend and she got herself a job serving in the bar and expected our relationship to blossom, and a British passport to be the end goal. Little did she realize that six weeks later she would find herself in 'Dumps Ville', as I did a tactical withdrawal from the cay.

After my time on the cay I returned to Airport Camp and settled into my last few weeks in the training wing. There were no major units coming over so other than a few survival courses being run out in the jungle, time was spent chilling on the beach and even a trip up to Cancun in Mexico to witness the famous American College break there. I then received the good news that I had been promoted to sergeant.

I had tried to get another extension to my posting but the battalion had seen me first-hand in this environment and had realized I was having way too much fun so I was under orders to return as soon as possible to the battalion.

CHAPTER EIGHT

Pray for what you want, but work for the things you need. - author unknown

THE COMMANDING OFFICER AT the time was a good man but as mad as a hatter. He reminded me of Basil Fawlty and had legs as long as my body and by God he could run. I was no slouch but I preferred to beast myself in the gym rather than on the tarmac; the CO on the other hand loved to run and would assess his men on their ability to keep up with him. I still remember the first run that he took me out on, the pain still fresh in my mind. He would do a five- or six-mile run at a steady pace with those fit enough to take part from the battalion and as we would approach the camp gates he would inform the RSM to take all but the NCOs away. A speech on how we had to be fitter than the men we led would ensue and then threats of how he would sack anyone who didn't keep up with him. This was a man who ran marathons for a hobby and as he bounded away I was at full sprint and was losing ground fast. My only saving grace was I was fitter than a lot of those around me and what I lacked in overall speed I made up for in stamina. An hour later, as I approached the gates of the camp the RSM stood there with the CO glaring at us. I could see myself being sacked and sent to the Officers Mess as a waiter for my poor performance. As I drew level the RSM grunted something at me and indicated that I should move to the right-hand side of the guardroom along with about thirty other tired looking members of the battalion. A short time after I had entered the camp the CO told the RSM to close the gates and made all those who hadn't come in on time to get in three ranks, before screaming obscenities at their lack of fitness and reasons for being in the army. Names were taken and all of them were placed on a three-month report with the threat of demotion and being sacked the reason for them to get fit. The bollocking was not just for their benefit and I made a mental note to get some extra miles in during the week to ensure that I was never that side of the gate. Even today I am amazed at how many fat and unfit people manage to slide through the net and get away with being unfit slobs in a job that dictates you have to be fit to do it properly. How some of those people can look in the mirror in the morning with pride God only knows.

I had not been a senior NCO long at this time and was still on a bit of a high from the added stature and pay that went with it. I had myself a nice little double room in the Warrant Officers and Sergeants Mess and life was looking up. My time with Recce Platoon was coming to a close and the CO had informed me that I was to go to Brecon and complete the platoon sergeants' battle course before taking over a rifle platoon in A Company. I had never wanted to do Senior Brecon and the bullshit that I went through during my section commanders course at Brecon was still among the bad memories etched in my mind. The army is not a democratic organization and with the CO's stamp on it I was going whether I liked it or not. I was thirty-two years old and the thought of being treated like a piece of shit did not lie well with me. With a few weeks to go before the start of the course I upped my running and got my head into the infantry pamphlets.

Dering Lines in Brecon is the school of excellence for the infantry. Anyone who is anybody in the infantry will have to pass through here at least twice, if not three times during their military career. All infantry career courses are run here from platoon commanders, platoon sergeants and section commanders battle courses to sniper and machine gun as well as company sergeant major courses. As well as all these main subjects they also run Territorial and range management courses; it's basically a busy place. As well as a busy place it's also a battle camp and everybody has to run everywhere. It was like being back in basic training except I was thirty-two years old and didn't appreciate the bullshit or shouting. The first main introduction for the course was held in a huge lecture room called the Falklands Hall where all 200 of us were told we were on a senior qualification course and we would all be treated like adults. That sounded good. Twenty minutes later we were being run at a fast pace to the other side of the camp for our first lesson, and this is how it would go for the next three months. We would muster every day before first light on the main square and be given vast amounts of ammunition, radios and rations, told to pack everything away and under shouts of ridicule and haste by the DS, given command appointments for the day; or 'disappointments' as we knew them. Code books and map co-ordinates were passed out to the chosen few, quick briefs given and then off we went to Sennybridge training area, which was about an hour's drive away, and we all believed it was twinned with a small corner of Hell.

You never knew what to expect weather-wise and as you passed the infamous cattle grid leading onto the training area it did its own thing; and what it did best here was rain. I know they say it isn't training until it's raining but this place took the piss, literally, even the sheep looked depressed. The course was aimed at training you as a platoon sergeant in a conventional warfare scenario, which meant that you carried a lot of weight over long distances and did a lot of blank and live firing attacks. Most of the course was spent in the field and the way they tested you and to see who had what it took to be a platoon sergeant, was to put you under pressure. The easiest way to do this was by sleep deprivation, and then, when you were mentally and physically tired, give you command appointments for even more pressure. If you were lucky you would get your command appointment early on in the week when everyone was quite fresh and willing to work for you. If your appointment fell in the second half of the week when everyone was knackered you were screwed, as you found yourself having to motivate yourself as well as those individuals around you.

The difference between the soldiers from different units on the course was immense. Some infantry line units had some excellent and very professional soldiers while other units sent shockingly bad people forward. It was almost like putting a clapped-out MOT failure car on the front courtyard of a Porsche garage. Brecon was where you were selected by your battalion to go on a prestige course and show the rest of the infantry world the kind of soldiers your battalion had to offer. Some of the guys on the course were so bad I had to wonder how they even managed to get through a junior NCO's course, let alone be let loose here. It would always wind me up when the Parachute Regiment guys would go on about how elite they were. Yes, they were fitter as a whole unit and they were very proud of their unit, almost to the verge of being brainwashed; but at the end of the day they were just infantry soldiers who could jump out of an aircraft if needed. I would take great satisfaction when I finished ahead of any of the Paras on the runs or long Bergen marches.

As on my earlier visit to Brecon, the course was broken into two distinct phases, one being the tactics phase and the other being the skill-at-arms phase. The tactics part of the course included a week of fitness and lectures followed by attack week. This was followed by defence, patrol and then offensive operations weeks. The phases meant little to all of us being taught and tested, all we knew was each day involved early starts in horrible weather conditions and the constant pressure in and out of command. As with everything we did, it was basic soldiering with lots of blank and live firing.

The attack week would always start in the platoon harbour area with a set of orders and then we would shake out in our patrol formations and through a series of report lines start our advance to contact across the training area. The wind and rain always seemed to be battering at our faces and the ground always seemed to be a severe drop or a mountainous ascent. When the enemy contacted us suppressive fire was laid down and quick battle orders (QBOs) were issued to tired and exhausted camouflaged faces. Indirect fire was directed onto enemy positions and assaulting sections were manoeuvred into place. Once the assault began depth positions were always encountered and the process of suppression and QBOs all began again. This would go on repetitively until the DS were happy that the individuals being tested had proved themselves up to the grade, and then there would be a slight lull in the battle as 'disappointments' were re-issued and the enemy had occupied their new defensive positions. The attacks would go on through the day and into the darkness before moving into patrol harbours in any one of the thick coniferous woods, where a new tasking would be issued. These would be anything from route recces to ambushes and night-fighting patrols. It was exhausting work and as the course progressed we were operating in robot mode, tiredness making even the most mundane task difficult; it was hard to focus on anything for long. You would not dare to close your eyes even for the briefest of moments as you knew you would be woken by angry shouts or a boot against the side of your head.

We were released from Dering Lines every Friday night and told to report back by Sunday evening to prepare for the following week, and although most of the course would don their disco dancing kit and head into Brecon town centre I found all I could be bothered to do was shower and collapse on my bed and sleep the sleep of a dead man. I could remember the days I could work and party with no problem, but at thirty-two years old I was finding it hard to battle through the aches and pains and tiredness. I would never grow old gracefully but if I was tired then it was time for bed, and on Sundays when the guys crawled in knackered and hung over to start the next week I felt better in myself.

The tactics phase was eventually over and after a long weekend we were into the skill-at-arms part of the course. Unlike the tactics phase, where we were tested physically and mentally, we were now taught and tested in our abilities to plan, conduct and manage everything to do with live firing ranges and field firing ranges as well as battle lessons. I managed to get a very good pass on the tactics course and finished high in the top third but I found it hard to concentrate on this phase. It was all range instruction writing, and shitty range traces day after day. One small smudge and your work would be red lined with a big fat "F", with the explanation from the jobsworth Small Arms School Corp instructor that a smudge was a safety error. Whatever! What the skill-at-arms phase did mean was that we could all hit the town and try out our charms on the local female population of Brecon.

Brecon is a small Welsh market town nestled into the southern end of the rolling scenic hills of central Wales. The population doubles on weekends with an influx of women coming in from the local towns as well as further afield, like Cardiff and Newport. On parade was Britain's finest, who hadn't had a drink in weeks and would buy drinks for any young or old bird that talked to them. Needless to say most of the 'Totty' on parade was far from appealing, but after a few beers most became approachable, and any regrets were lost until the following morning when the results were laid next to you. I finished both phases of the course in the top third and I was pleased with my performance but at thirty-two my body was feeling the effects of long physical activity and the stress that went with it. I looked forward to taking a chill pill and a few weeks of inactivity back at the battalion. How wrong could I have been.

On my return to the battalion I was congratulated by the RSM and the CO on my performance throughout the course and then told I was now officially out of the Recce Platoon and was to report to my new job in the training wing, where I would work until there was a slot for me as platoon sergeant. I was gutted that I was no longer a part of the Recce Platoon but was looking forward to the change of direction in my career. Unfortunately, the change of direction I had hoped for was to go straight in as a platoon sergeant but it looked like I would have to wait a while for that to happen.

The training wing in camp was a shoddy unimpressive building with a series of unimpressive classrooms and a main lobby area. There was a sergeant major in overall charge but he had been gone for over three months to Belize, setting up the battalion's future exercises out there. There was a private soldier who had worked there so long he was part of the furniture and would prove invaluable to me as he knew all the procedures involved in the job. My first task was to set up a Tactics Cadre for the up-and-coming future lance corporals who were waiting to go on their section commanders course at Brecon. Obviously having just returned from there I was the natural choice to prepare these guys for their course.

I spent about five months in the training wing and enjoyed my time there. I was my own boss most of the time and busy and stress were words of the past. Then, out of the blue one day, I was called in to see the CO and he informed me I would be taking over from the current platoon sergeant of 1 Platoon, A Company. I was over the moon as that was where I had started my career as a private soldier. The training wing job had been good but it was a holding place and it wasn't good to spend time there if you wanted to progress further. A Company was currently out in Kabul, Afghanistan. They were there as part of the International Security Assistance Force (ISAF), and were doing the first three and a half months of a seven-month tour the battalion had picked up. Our B Company would relieve them at the halfway point.

My flight out to Afghanistan was by a Hercules transport aircraft and six other soldiers from the battalion joined me on the flight. There were only stores on the aircraft so we all found an area of flooring and stretched out for the flight. Five hours into the flight and one of the RAF flight crew told us to retake our seats as we would be making an unexpected overnight stop in Bucharest, Romania. Unlike the army, the RAF were much more laid back and grown up with their approach to how they treated people on stopovers. The army would put a thousand restrictions in place before anyone had even done anything wrong; the RAF on the other hand just gave a report time to be back at the hotel the next day. A coach picked us up from the airport and took us to a five-star hotel in downtown Bucharest; what a stroke of luck. The only problem being we had not expected this stop and had brought no civilian clothing to wear, so out came the regimental track suit and Silver Shadow running trainers and we were off. There looked to be a few good bars but with only one night to explore the city there was only one place to see the real Bucharest, the strip bars and red light district. The area was dingy and cheap and the old Soviet influence was everywhere; however, the women were attractive and the beer was cold and with four months of sweaty hairy soldiers ahead of us this was paradise. Late the next morning we kicked out our new found girlfriends from our rooms, with looks of disgust from the female receptionists, and made our way to the transport and our onward flight to Afghanistan.

CHAPTER NINE

The happiest of people don't necessarily have the best of everything; they just make the most of everything that comes their way. - Karen S. Magee

FOR ME AND EVERYONE who ever came to Kabul, or anywhere else in Afghanistan, it was a massive shock. On the transport to Camp Souter, which was to be our home for our time here, we passed what can only be described as the biggest shit hole I had ever seen. When I arrived at the camp, I was greeted by the outgoing platoon sergeant who could not hide his delight that I was here, and he would soon be heading back to the UK. I had a one week handover of kit and equipment as well as area familiarization before being thrown in at the deep end, leading my platoon on operations in Afghanistan. As a platoon sergeant I had twenty-eight men under my command, broken down into seven four-man teams. There was no platoon commander in place when I arrived as the old one had returned to the UK on a posting, but a new one was inbound. When he arrived the new platoon commander was straight from the Royal Military Academy at Sandhurst. At twenty-four he was older than most of the new platoon commanders that turned up. He came to the platoon with a posh accent and an attitude I would have to break later.

Patrolling in the Kabul area was broken down into vehicle and foot patrols with each of the two multiples in the platoon doing ten hours a day on the ground. These hours were split down to six hours with the vehicle and four on foot. I learned early that to be dropped off on a patrol tasking without your vehicles in intimate support meant you had no communications, and to be miles away from base location, on foot and with no communications, was asking for trouble. The southern part of our area of responsibility (AOR) was Police District 9, which was an urban interface. The other area we patrolled was Police District 8, which was a more rural area. The most remote area, District 9, was a nightmare for establishing communications back to headquarters and even when you were on foot it was hard to even keep communications between our teams within the multiple unless you were within line of sight of each other. Each of the company's three platoons would do six weeks of patrolling and then move on to guards and QRF duties followed by a training cycle, where most of the time you ended up either back on patrols or boosting up the quick reaction force. We had free run for most of the time to plan our own platoon patrol matrix and as long as we did the hours on the ground and covered both police districts the head shed left us alone. I would always take our FFR (fitted for radio) Land Rover on any patrol tasking as it had the best radios with the longest range, so we could reach back to headquarters. The second vehicle we would always take was our Wimic; this was a stripped down Land Rover with either a fifty calibre machine gun or in our case our tried and tested GPMGs, mounted for extra fire power.

As with all the training you do in the British Army before deploying on operations, you expect that you are going into a war zone once you finally get there. When you drive out of the camp gates for the first time you wait expectantly for small arms fire and rocket propelled grenades (RPGs) to start raining down upon you. What actually happens is that people smile and wave at you and small children engulf your vehicles asking for chocolates and sweets; there didn't seem to be any hard or bad feelings anywhere. It took a few patrols to get the feel for the area and to get to know the short cuts around the various police districts. We would try to take an Afghan police officer with us on our patrols as often as we could so they could deal with any minor incidents that were not linked with terrorism. We would never inform the coppers we were coming to pick them up as this could lead to a nasty little surprise being left for us in the shape of an ambush or an improvised explosive device (IED) planted alongside the road. Instead we would drive up to the police stations and get the interpreter to go in and grab any free copper that was ready to go out with us on patrol. Unlike the Americans who would drive by in their armoured Hummer Jeeps at 60 mph through the little villages we would get out and patrol on foot, remove our sun glasses and talk to the people. It gave us a chance to get up close and personal to the local population and with the use of the interpreter we would discuss local problems with the relevant tribal leaders. This also gave us the atmospherics of an area which again you could not get from within the confines of a vehicle. The whole way of life for the Afghan people was tribal loyalties and their religion and to insult either of these was to insult them and their families.

Corruption in Afghanistan was everywhere, from the government, to the army and police. They could not be trusted. The poverty was so deep rooted and had been for so long the people took it as a sign from Allah that they were to live like this. There were numerous international projects being set up to improve their standard of living, like getting the power stations back on line for electricity, but they were not concerned. Most of the houses were self-built mud huts and their sewers ran straight from the house along with the rubbish into the street where it rotted and dried up. When we first got there we would take up kneeling firing positions whenever we stopped but that was soon binned when we saw human faeces everywhere. The stench that hung around everywhere was outrageous and the small children would be playing among the piles of rotting rubbish. The hanging carcasses of goats and cows with their throats cut would be left to bleed by the sides of the roads, their bodies covered with swarms of flies. When people wanted some meat they would have chunks cut off here and there. How they never developed severe food poisoning I don't know.

We would patrol the small villages that resembled something out of the distant past, untouched by the twenty-first century; many of the local people still used donkeys and carts as their main means of transport. As poor as the people were, they would still go out of their way to be friendly to us. No matter where we went, they would invite us in for tea. We were told to decline these offers as the water was unclean and the majority of the time not boiled properly. We got around it by asking them to use our water to make it. The Afghan tea was an acquired taste, it was given in a small glass, very strong and with huge lumps of crystallized sugar that gave it the consistency of syrup. It wasn't the greatest cuppa in the world but when you got used to the idea they were using your water and it was only a small glass, you would all sit there cross legged on their Persian rugs and discuss, through the aid of the interpreter, everything from the lack of electricity, to the possible movements of insurgents or smugglers in the area. We were only too aware that although they were outwardly friendly towards us, you could also sense their stand-offish attitude.

About half way through our tour we were tasked with setting up a series of observation posts (OPs) on a small ridge of hills that looked down onto one of the mountain passes into Kabul. It was believed that some of the local criminal gangs were smuggling weapons and drugs through the pass and into the city market places and beyond. The operation was to have my platoon mount the six observation posts as a forward screen and trigger other teams from the company who kept out of sight and triggered our QRFs onto any activity we observed. Attached to us for the operation was a troop of Dutch Recce soldiers. They were reported to be good professional guys who in their world were classed as the country's elite troops. I had recced the area of the operation a few days previously and the day before we were to go in I gathered all those that would be going together and gave a set of detailed orders and rehearsals.

We left at around midnight to the various drop-off points and as we sat in the back of our non-armoured 4-tonne truck we scanned the area around us with our night sights and thermal imagery to ensure there was neither enemy nor anyone else who might give away our position. With the coast clear we debussed from the truck and melted into the night, waiting for the vehicles to move off and the local dogs to stop barking. With the night settled and quiet again I did a quick navigation check and moved off on the first leg of our insertion to our OP position, only to stop again within 300 metres as one of the Dutch soldiers went over on his ankle. With the Dutch soldier eventually casevaced by the QRF call sign we continued on the monstrous climb to the summit of the mountain where our OP was to be situated. It was apparent that by 0500 hrs the morning dawn was going to catch us short of the summit and out in the open, we had no choice but to find a cluster of rocks and nestle down out of sight for the day. The heat of the day was intense and we had to ensure we were not compromised so we just lay still and sweated our bodies away into the rocks we lay on, watching the local population carry on with their daily crappy lives, completely unaware that British soldiers were watching them from the hills above.

That night we carried on up the mountain pass and inserted into our OP, tired but thankful we were finally there, the weight of our packs and the heat having drained us to our very limits. The Dutch soldiers proved to be a hardy, professional bunch and any doubts I might have had about them before had been replaced by respect. With our intimate security placed out and the various optical sights we had trained onto the target area, we got into a routine of sentry and observer, while the remainder of the patrol either rested or carried out administrative tasks. As the next day approached I listened as the other patrols radioed in on their scheduled windows and gave headquarters their situation reports (sit-reps). I was shocked and angry to learn that of the six patrols that had inserted only three had reached their OP positions without being compromised and three had been picked up and extracted back to base location.

It was on day two that we noticed movement of men and equipment about three kilometres away on the forward-facing slope of a rocky ridge line. Our optics were not that good at that distance to focus in on too much detail but we could make out they were military. I asked the platoon commander for a grid of his location as he was the closest team to the activity but he said he was too far away to react. When he was asked to move to the location to investigate the movement he refused, giving as his reason that he believed there were mines in that area. With no other way of finding out what was going on, I tasked the QRF to move in and get eyes on. I guided them into the area and when the answer came back I thought I would explode. As the QRF had moved into the area the first thing they had noticed was an unmanned Minimi machine gun. As the Afghans had no Minimis the alarm bells were ringing in my head. A little further on they came to a GPMG with a sleeping sentry next to it; an A Company sleeping sentry. One of my guys! The platoon commander was found further up with the remainder of the patrol, all asleep. He had given me the wrong grid and had then not listened to the radio as we moved the QRF onto his position. Unprofessional wankers! The worst part of it was it would have been easy to have gone aggressive by use of indirect fire or fast air against what we thought was insurgent activity and instead took out our own guys with a Blue on Blue incident. Mr Fucking Dick Head, the platoon commander, would receive a right hook on return to camp.

When he had arrived in Afghanistan this particular platoon commander had been the subject of one of the best stitch ups I had ever seen, one that went on for over three weeks. On the first Orders Group (O group) he attended, which were held daily by the CO, he was told to sit back and listen but say nothing. If he had any questions he was to ask me afterwards. As we sat there the CO pulled out a small foil package, unwrapped it and placed it in the middle of the table. In it was foot powder, but it looked like drugs and he made out it was just in from our Afghan dealers on the border, with the further shipment of twenty kilos on the way and the money from this shipment reaching our bank accounts by the end of the month. The look of shock on the PC's face was evident but to give him credit he didn't say anything and even at later O groups he kept quiet. This kept on for three weeks with weapons, ammunition and more imitation drugs being shown and details of imaginary shipments for sale being given; even a Royal Military Police (RMP) man was present to give the stitch up more credibility. It was a perfect set up and on the third week some of the RMPs who had not been present on the O groups took the said platoon commander in for questioning on corruption and dodgy dealings within the company. They wanted a snitch and convinced the platoon commander he was the man to take those responsible in the company down. With the breaking strain of a Kit Kat, he named everyone he thought was responsible in the company. Good bloke! The next day on the daily O group the RMP made a guest appearance and played the tape of him stitching everyone up, to his absolute horror. If he ever got captured by the Taliban we were screwed, they would know the colour of our pants by the time they had finished with him.

As with all long operational tours when you are single, you would start writing to pen pals, as I did. I would choose a few likely girls from the various Internet sites and get spinning my yarns. It wasn't long before emails and letters started coming in and the job of whittling them down began. I would ask for photographs and those who never sent any, with whatever lame excuses, would be binned; this would mean they were probably mingers. If they said they had bubbly personalities or liked to stay in and watch films they were fat, so they were binned. By the time I came to the end of my tour I had narrowed my list down to three likely targets and with my conversations with two of them I was fairly certain I was in for a good time during my R&R. I was soon to find out though that these women lied as much as I did.

While on tour lots of the guys hit the gym and when I took over the platoon I made fitness one of my top priorities. I soon had most of the platoon doing regular workouts and runs and when the CO and RSM came out to visit they commented on the fact that they had seen a lot of the guys working out. The CO also pointed out that I needed to ensure the men could still run as this was his priority. I looked him in the eye and told him that we would all be so big by the end of the tour we would never have to run anywhere again. I was joking but he took it seriously and when I mentioned that chicks loved big blokes he shook his head and moved off. Short visit.

Life in Camp Souter was not that bad considering our surroundings. We had the best food and accommodation of all the multinational forces based in the area and although the patrols programme was quite intense you knew what you were doing most of the time and there was little to no bullshit added. It didn't seem to us we were making a damn bit of difference to the country and as usual we did not think there was a valid reason to be here; but as the saying goes, ours is not to reason why, merely to do and die. Well, hopefully not die anyway. The bright side was after every tour there was a wad of money in the bank and the opportunity to act like a rock star for a while. Like I have said, the local population were friendly enough and it was easy to become complacent and let your guard down, and that is exactly what happened to the Germans.

I had my guys on QRF duty on the normal rotation and had just come off Ops room duty when a call came across the radio asking for assistance to a German call sign that had been hit on the main supply route (MSR), about half a kilometre from our camp. Unlike the Germans, we always changed our routes and timings to avoid terrorist actions being planned against us but unfortunately the Germans had become complacent and had set patterns, and because of that they got hit, and hit hard. An old green bus taking the German bomb disposal teams back to Kabul Airport at the end of their tour in Afghanistan had been targeted. They were using the same route at the same time as they always did for this run and hadn't noticed the taxi following them, which then pulled alongside and detonated 250 kilograms of explosive.

By the time the QRF force got there they were greeted by a scene of carnage that was straight out of a horror film, with the bus blown off the road and into a nearby field. There had been thirty-four smiling happy Germans on that bus and every one of them was seriously messed up with four of them paying the ultimate sacrifice and dying. There were limbs and bits of people everywhere and some were reaching for pictures of their loved ones or crying out their names to help them. It was horrific and to add to the chaos there was a gathering crowd who were chanting and laughing. A stray dog had even picked up a piece of torn flesh and run off with it. The guys were close to emptying their magazines into the crowd, and the dog, but it was calmed down and the gruesome job of giving first aid was continued. The dead and injured were taken to multinational military hospitals around the Kabul area and a few were even taken to Camp Souter, a timely reminder for us there that this was a dangerous place.

The fifteen-second Sky News report later that day reported that four Germans were killed in an explosion in Kabul. Nothing about the other thirty soldiers that would spend the rest of their lives without their arms and legs or half their faces blown away. The weather had more coverage.

The platoon was deeply traumatized by the incident with the Germans and I was not sure how to deal with the tears and disturbed soldiers. Sympathy was never my strong point and the best way to deal with this was to get permission to have the bar open and the drinking rules relaxed for the day. With the welfare people and the padre at hand the guys got drunk. There was a lot of guilt and then anger as to what we were doing here and who was responsible, all of which I had no answer to. If there was a face to this enemy it would have been easier but the enemy was hidden and faceless, as was the case in all the conflicts we were in at this stage.

The next day we were back on patrol again and we made a point of passing through the area where the Germans had been hit the day before. The bus had been removed from the scene but the crater in the road and the dark dried out blood stains were a grim reminder of the dangers this crappy country held.

A couple of weeks later we were tasked with moving up to a large ridge line that dominated Police District 9 and show a presence there as suspicious movement had been seen, we needed to find out if it was terrorist or friendly. The dusty track that meandered up the steep ridge was not for the faint hearted, and as we neared the top the drop was over 2,000 feet straight down. The view over Kabul and the surrounding country side was amazing and we could just make out the area where a Dutch call sign had been hit a few days before and lost one of their men and the interpreter. At the summit a small group of Afghan soldiers sat on an old Persian rug drinking tea; they had no vehicles and no radios. They waved us over and after the normal introductions we sat with them and drank sweet tea. They had been tasked with watching all movement at the base of the ridge below. They didn't know how long they were going to be there and had no means of telling anyone if they did see anything. We said our farewells and mounted up on our vehicles before carrying on along the ridge line. A couple of kilometres further on we came across another group of Afghan militia soldiers, but these were different from the last group. They had sentries out that moved down the track to cut us off and behind them were depth positions manned by alert soldiers, all with their rifles pointing in our direction. Both our vehicles were in single file on a small track with no room for manoeuvre and a large drop to one side, the arcs of fire were limited due to the front vehicle being in line with the Afghan soldiers. We were at a huge disadvantage. I warned everyone by whisper over the radio to be ready to engage on my call and with the interpreter I debussed from the vehicle and made my way towards the waiting Afghans. The leader of the Afghan force was speaking into a radio which was unusual and as he put the hand set down he moved down to meet us.

As he approached I told the interpreter to stay behind me as that way I could see if he was being intimidated and to only say what I told him to say as they had a tendency to waffle on and you had no way of knowing what was being said. I needed to control all aspects of the conversation as things could go wrong fast if not done correctly. I asked the commander for access straight away along the track and reminded him I was part of the British Army and the International Security Assistance

Force here in Kabul and had right of way. His eyes hardened and I could see straight away that he was not going to allow us access and this was further backed up as he shouted for his men to bring their weapon systems to bear onto us. I had to act quickly as this was a situation that was slipping from my grasp fast so I called through the PRR (personal role radio) for my guys to bring their weapons to bear and look for the nearest bit of cover if this went any further. At the same time I demanded to know the Afghan commander's name and the unit he was with. We were on the worst possible place to be if it went wrong but I had to put on an aggressive attitude as this was the only thing these people respected. Weakness now would spell disaster for us. The answer he gave sent a shiver down my spine; it was the Afghan Chief of Defence, the most corrupt warlord in Afghanistan. As well as being the Chief of Defence he also had his own personal army of 28,000 troops who looked after his own interests: land, drugs and weapons to name but a few. With his personal interests and the position he held in the government, plus the money he received from the Americans for helping on the war on terror he was a powerful man indeed. As much as I wanted to push this issue and move through his shitty little check point he had the upper hand so with a stark warning given that I would return with a company of British troops later that evening I motioned for the vehicles to reverse down the slope and away from the check point. As I headed back to camp I was livid but also relieved, it could have all gone horribly wrong with either an international incident with our so-called Afghan friends or even worse, casualties. Later that evening when the company commander told me that I should have 'gone for it' I reminded him it was the commander's call on the ground, and if I had pushed it and any of our guys had died maybe he wouldn't have been so enthusiastic to have said that I should have 'gone for it'. I never did like that prick!

When we came back in from patrol to Camp Souter there was a chicane system and thick chains to negotiate before you reached the relative safety of the camp. This was to stop would-be suicide car- and truck-bombers getting in and detonating within the perimeter defences and causing mass casualties like with the Americans in Beirut that killed over 200 of their troops. It was a lengthy process that had to be endured and we would normally turn off the radio systems once it was reported we were back in base location and the troops would make their way to the unloading bays leaving the vehicles and commanders to be searched. On this day as we came through the chicane system we turned off the radios and the troops debussed, ready to make their way to the unloading bay when there was a huge explosion in the outward bound traffic lane. As per standard operating procedure (SOP) we took cover and donned our helmets. I went to send a contact report but the radio had been turned off and it took time to turn it back on and re-tune it so we mounted up and spun the vehicles around and headed back out of camp. This is where we all looked like some comedy outtake as we still didn't know exactly what had happened. I presumed we had received some sort of indirect fire attack. At the front sandbagged sanger (defensive position) I shouted up to the sentry who had taken cover on the floor where the attack had come from, he didn't know but said it had been a grenade attack. With no radio communications and no direction I made the decision to go left down towards the main MSR, two vehicles and no dismounts. The remainder of the platoon under one of the NCOs on seeing us bomb burst out the front gate had made his decision to take the rest of the platoon out of the side gate of the camp and had almost run into the escaping grenade thrower as he sprinted for the safety of the urban environment, a couple of hundred metres away. One of the guys ended up rugby tackling him to the ground where the insurgent got a justified couple of digs and kicks for his struggling efforts

As we gathered up the platoon and escorted the prisoner back to camp the place was in uproar. He was taken off us straight away and taken for tactical questioning while the shock of capture had him on the back foot. It wasn't long before he started giving his story. Apparently he was from the north of Afghanistan and had travelled down to Kabul in the hope of finding work. When the reality of finding no work had sunk in he was approached by unknown persons who had given him two hundred US dollars and the promise of martyrdom as well as his family being looked after once he attacked and killed some British soldiers. He was given a grenade and a lift to the area of the camp by motor cycle and told to wait for a patrol to pass, that patrol was us returning to camp. He had run to the side of the camp wall and lobbed the grenade over the wall to the area he thought we would be. Luckily for us it landed in the outgoing lane which was divided by a thick Hesco Bastion wall. His arms and body had pen-written messages all over it: Death to the Infidels (us) and he was going to a better place. What a psycho! As it was we handed him over to the Afghan police and a few days later they shot him. Justice, Afghan style!

We had two weeks left of our tour and on one of the daily briefs we were informed of a large amount of handicapped people being sent to Kabul from all around Afghanistan to be used as suicide bombers. We had not suffered from the scourge of suicide bombers like other places and the thought of waves of them coming into Kabul was scary. To add to that was the fact they were thinking of using mentally and physically handicapped people to carry out these attacks. It goes against everything that is right.

In Kabul the main roads were covered with huge speed bumps that are about three times bigger than those we get in the UK, leaving you no option but to slow down when you approach them. This is where all the beggars and tradesmen would ply their business to the mass of slowed traffic, including us. If they were to hit us here they would have almost stationary targets that were all non-armoured. It would be a killing area that would be hard to counter. The company commander made the decision that we would surge onto the main routes leading into Kabul and place vehicle check points (VCPs). This was a shit plan as far as I was concerned and I made my opinion known, to deaf ears. For us to sit on the side of a road waiting for these potential bombers to come into Kabul was crazy. If they were stopped they would detonate early, taking out anyone in the area with them. The OC said we had to stop them getting to the camp, if that was one of their targets, and yet the camp was better prepared for an attack than our Land Rovers. The OC finished his brief by saying it was his decision as a commander and if someone died today he would take the responsibility of informing loved ones. It was the most un-motivational speech I had ever heard. My mum would have kicked his arse if she had heard it.

There was no way I was going to sit on some road and wait for some mental retard to pre-detonate his vest and turn us all into red mist. With a "Yes, sir" and a smart about turn I briefed up the platoon on what would really happen that day. We had survived this far on the tour by not being stupid so I was not about to start now. The first thing we did was make sure we did not stop at any of the speed bumps and then made our way to a scenic green area near one of the larger rivers in the area. We got ourselves in all round defence and chilled in the Afghan sun. When a local farmer came along we got the interpreter to offer him some rations for a go on his horse and donkey. A few good hours of horse and donkey races then began, with a dip in the river to finish off a good day of VCP duty.

The final few days consisted of taking the incoming company soldiers around the area of operations and endless briefings. My final view of Afghanistan was blocked out as the tail ramp came up on the Hercules transport plane, and then it was just noise as we headed back to the UK. Both my arms and legs were still in place so it had been a successful tour.

CHAPTER TEN

Oh, Lord, please keep my Soldier tonight,
Close by Your guiding hand of might.
Give him the strength to carry on
When all is dark and hope is gone.
Help him to trust and have no fear
For You are watching, ever near.
Let him know he's not alone;
Your light will always lead him home.
He's rough and tough, no emotions shown
But, God, he's just a boy, You know.
He claims the title and wears it proud;
Says he's the best and says it loud.
And though someday he'll guard Your heights,
Lord, please bring him safely home tonight.

- author unknown

RETURNING TO THE UK in the summer of 2003 was a massive anticlimax for me. As a platoon sergeant out on ops in Afghanistan my guys were mine and everyone would leave us alone to get on with the job. The patrol matrix we were given had to be adhered to but how you went about your business was your problem and I had the final say in most platoon matters. Now we were back in Chepstow everything we did was scrutinized and I couldn't do anything with my platoon unless cleared with the company sergeant major (CSM) and OC. If I wanted to take the guys out for a run then it had to fit in with the company training programme; if I wanted to take the guys out on one of the exercise areas or ranges I had to give them six weeks notice and then it had to fit in with the training programme. Every day I would find most of my time taken up by briefings and inspections and basically standing around waiting for nothing. It was one of the most frustrating times of my career and I hated these days, and longed to be back in Afghanistan.

To relieve this frustration I rang up my pen pals and made arrangements to meet them; not at the same time obviously. The first of my Internet girlfriends I decided to meet lived in London and I arranged to meet her in neutral territory, the scenic city of Bath. It was close enough to drive and far enough from Chepstow in case I had to do an emergency bug out. I had a faded photo of her but it left a lot to go wrong, like she hadn't told me how much she weighed or if she had all her toes or was she inbred with five thumbs. Being the brave soldier I was I ventured into enemy territory not knowing whether this would be a successful mission or not. She had pre-booked a room for us in a little bed-and-breakfast and gave me directions to the pub where she would be waiting for me. With my imagination all over the place I made my way to the B&B, collected the room key and dropped my bag next to hers in the room. What I should have done was opened her bag and checked out the size of her pants to confirm whether it was worth going any further but instead I dumped my bag and walked to the pub. I had thought that my final get-out clause would be to blend into the crowd in the pub and check her out from afar, if she ended up being a 'Hippo' then I would pop smoke and leg it. As it was I entered a pub that had the atmosphere of a morgue, and the clientele of a special needs clinic. There was the barman, me and a swamp thing in the corner. The swamp thing looked at me and I froze; maybe she hadn't seen me. She waved and then stood up and wallowed towards me. I thought I would scream but instead just grimaced. It was clothed in what can only be described as a black curtain that at some stage must have covered a big window in a big house and she must have had massive back problems, as her tits were huge. She took me to a table and ordered me a pint of lager which I downed in one and listened to her say how glad she was I had turned up; I nodded numbly and ordered the barman to keep the pints coming. She had lied to me about everything, the photograph I had been sent was definitely not the swamp thing that sat before me. Oh well, I had made my bed and now I had to lie in it.

The next morning as she lay sleeping I crept out of the room and sprinted to my car, and with tyres screeching headed back to Chepstow and the security of an armed guard on the main gate of camp with orders left to shoot to kill the swamp monster if she decided to follow. The barrage of missed calls and voice mails saying she was going to kill me left no choice but for me to dump my phone and get a new one. With number one girlfriend crossed off my list I moved down to number two and arranged to meet her in Bristol, she sounded a lot nicer, and smaller. This time I brought a friend as back up in case it all went horribly wrong again. The rendezvous was yet another pub and a description of what she would be wearing was given, black leather mini skirt with pink leather high boots. My God, I must have hit the jackpot here, she sounded awesome.

As my mate and I entered the busy pub we made our way to the counter and ordered a couple of beers, hoping I would get eyes on the target first. The only person that I could see wearing black and pink however was a monster in the corner with a group of girlfriends, please don't let it be her I remember thinking. A huge fat hand slapping my arse nearly lifted me off the floor. Oh my God, she had seen me. As she led me to one of the tables she sat me down on one of her knees and began stroking the back of my neck with her fat bratwurst fingers and went into graphic detail of what she was going to do to me later. I felt sick. How had this happened again? I was not going to be used like last time and after making out I had to go to the toilet made my way towards the back of the pub. Thankfully there was a back door and as I stepped out into an alleyway I ran. About two kilometres down the road I sat in a small pub, ordered a beer and sent a text to my mate saying that I would wait here for him. As it was he turned up with two of the other girls in tow, who were much nicer, and the night was not a total loss. On return to camp the next day I threw away my list of potential girlfriends and made a promise to never meet women online again.

A few days later I decided after a phone call from the girl I had met the other night to go meet her. The only problem was that it was about four in the morning and I was stinking drunk. Whatever brain cells I had were numbed to the point of being dead so I grabbed my car keys and headed down to Bristol for what was left of the night of pleasure. Within twenty minutes of driving I became drowsy and despite the music on full and the windows down I drifted off to sleep. I don't know how it happened but as I passed a truck in deep slumber on the outside lane, the sound of his horn and my car smashing into the central reservation woke me instantly. I was lucky I had connected exactly side on to the reservation with my car and as I bounced back into the motorway I put my foot down and headed to the nearest services for a tea and a sleep. I could so easily have died or killed somebody else that morning and I made a promise to myself to never drink and drive again.

Meanwhile, back in camp normal army life continued and when we did leave camp we would be sent out in section groups or anything up to company size taskings. These were normally crappy little jobs that would last for anything from a day to a month. As a platoon sergeant I got to take my guys down to Sandhurst and take part in the platoon commanders course urban exercise and then jump on the transport and head up to Brecon and prepare to be the enemy in their final tactical exercise. From here I would then head elsewhere in the country and do lessons for cadets or assist in Territorial exercises. It was a lot of travelling and time away but there was no bullshit and there were always piss-ups and time on the town. Not much proper soldiering though. On one such task I moved down to Lydd, near Folkestone which is where the army did its confirmatory live fire training for operations for UK-based soldiers. I was to head up part of the permanent range team (PRT) with a few other members of the company for an artillery unit that was being deployed to the Balkans.

Most of the troops that came through the range were okay but there was one troop commander that came through, a woman who had a chip on her shoulder. She shouted her orders at her guys like she was in the German SS; in fact she reminded me of my ex-wife. Everything was videoed and replayed for the troops as part of a hot debrief directly after each scenario was completed and she would stand there criticizing her guys with snide comments even though she wouldn't go down herself. The range itself was very good with streets and cars, as well as houses and mannequin talking dummies controlled through a link to the control tower.

She continued to send her junior commanders through but refused to go down herself, and as with a lot of sub-standard commanders, being put under pressure was not a welcome thought. We finally managed to convince her to go through as the last team of the day but she put a young private soldier in as commander being the good person she was. I chatted briefly to the range control in the tower and hatched my plan to catch her out. As her team were being briefed up on the patrol lane I took off all my clothes and ran out to one of the many parked cars on the range, taking with me a yellow wig and a newspaper. As the patrol left the base location I noticed she was the third person, which meant she was the chat-up person for the patrol; the plan should work. As the team moved towards the car I was sitting in, the control tower relayed instructions via their radio to the patrol that they should find out why this vehicle was parked here. The team all went to ground and as the chat-up person she approached the car. I had the wig on and the newspaper in front of me and from a distance I must have looked like one of the mannequins in the other cars. Little did she know she had a surprise in store for her. As she got to the window and leaned in to talk to the mannequin I dropped the newspaper and asked her what the problem was. The look of shock and confusion as she jumped back was priceless, her face then turned red in a blind rage as I tucked the newspaper under my arm and walked calmly past her and through the middle of the giggling patrol. When the range control played the tape back later that day everyone was on their backs in hysterics, everyone that is except Miss Prim and Proper who couldn't believe a senior NCO could behave so badly. Stuck up cow!!

Since joining the army, I had always been into my weights. It was a means to keep fit but also a way to release the tensions of the day. Some people ran, others read a book or listened to music; I blasted myself in the gym. I was never going to become the next Arnold Schwarzenegger as that would mean devoting your life to the sport. Diet and no drinking, lots of sleep and steroids! I had always been tempted but after seeing the side effects on one of my best mates I thought better of it. To use the stuff properly meant to use small doses and after six weeks come off it for two months or more before starting another six-week cycle. My mate, who had never been overly big or temperamental for that matter, turned into a complete lunatic over a very short period of time. He kept injecting with no rest period and bigger and bigger doses. His body and strength doubled but something in his head changed as well. His marriage crumbled and he was constantly fighting down town, the normally placid man now an enraged animal. While playing rugby for the battalion he was tackled and his leg shattered with the crack of a snapping branch. His weakened lower leg bones were broken in six separate locations. On release from hospital he carried on with the use of the steroids and bought himself a road racing motor cycle. One day he found himself doing 175 mph down the motorway wearing only his helmet and a thong as well as being drunk. I remember one day bumping into him down town. He was in fancy dress and drunk and by himself. He had decided to get dressed up as a woman and go out on the piss by himself. Hmm? As it was, after a serious bike accident which almost left him dead he turned to religion as a means to turn his life around. When I next visited him months later I walked into his local church to find him in a suit singing to the congregation. He was singing a song he had written himself about Jesus and was even playing the guitar. Later that evening he took me out about town and introduced me to all the homeless people he had befriended; he was a changed man - if not a bit weird.

It had been down at Lydd that one of the guys asked if I would like to meet his girlfriend's mother. Now, I may have enjoyed playing the field but I was not a granny grabber. I changed my mind when he described her though and later that day I sent a text message to a woman named Catherine. The text message went well and later on that evening after a few beers I developed enough Dutch courage to phone her. She was funny and mad all wrapped into one and I ended up asking her out for a beer, with directions that she would know it was me when I gave her the code words, "the man with the black moustache walks south for the winter". She would answer, "red fox", a normal person would have hung up at this stage but she laughed and said yes.

On my return from Lydd I made my plans to go and pick Catherine up and wondered at what I was doing. I had a kind of girlfriend down the road that I had met on the Bristol night but then again I didn't like her that much; she wasn't the brightest spark in the box. My track record recently on picking up chicks wasn't much to brag about either, she was bound to be fat, ugly or sectioned. I picked p Catherine up later that night as she was lighting up a cigarette while sitting on the local Tesco's garage fuel storage tanks and my code words went out the window as I nervously asked her if she wanted a lift. This was obviously a woman with a death wish. The evening went too fast and we talked as if we had to tell our life stories to each other before we parted that night. As I drove her home that evening we talked and laughed until all of a sudden she looked at me and told me to pull the car over to the side of the road as she wanted to kiss me. I wanted to slam the brakes on and take her in my arms then and there but played it cool and drove a little further down the road to a small pub where I said we could have a nightcap. As I pulled into the car park my heart was racing and I found myself nervous. What the hell was going on? She was only a woman who wanted a kiss, Why all the nerves? As I turned off the ignition I leant across and we kissed for the first time, it was slow and long and as we pulled away something changed between us and with a stupid grin on my face I led her into the pub for our nightcap.

A few days later her daughter, Saresh, handed me a small Mr Happy doll, from the Mr Men collection, followed by a big hug saying thanks for making her mum happy. Bargain! I might be in there after all. Things thereafter moved at quite a fast pace and we tried to see each other as often as possible. I made my excuses with my part-time girlfriend in Bristol and Catherine ended her relationship with her then ex. Things were looking up. She had never had much to do with military life and I was wary of bringing her into the mess with all its traditional rules. She was a loose cannon when it came to rules and the like. I started her off nice and easy and we became regulars at the 2003 World Cup Rugby tournament that was on at the time. Every weekend we would sit in the

Sergeants Mess and watch the tournament unfold to an amazing final where England came out triumphant against the massively favourite Australians.

From the rugby in the mess came the first mess do in the form of a fancy dress Warriors and Wenches evening. Despite my pleas for her to abide by the rules she turned up as Zena, the Warrior Princess, in the shortest leather miniskirt ever made. I pointed out the RSM and the CO to her and explained if she pissed them off I would be on regimental duties until I collected my pension, she answered this with a mischievous laugh and ran off toward the CO. I pictured my career ending instantly as Catherine had the confused looking CO manhandled onto the stage by a character called Max Blood Axe the Viking, before they pretended to disembowel him to cheers from the mess. This was early on in the night, before people were drunk and everyone thought it was funny, except the CO and the RSM, and of course a hiding Egyptian prince that was me. Later that evening as Catherine was jumping up and down on my knee to the music, another senior NCO was to receive extra duties mistakenly being identified as us. Apparently it looked like we were having sex and that was not becoming of behaviour in the mess.

The next function I dared bring Catherine to was the battalion's all-ranks do. We came as cowboy and cowgirl and, as normal, she wore the shortest shorts and the lowest cut top, I warned her it was winter and she would freeze but the Warrior Princess knew best and as the night got colder and the booze stronger and more plentiful she lost her eyesight and couldn't feel her legs. This was a common ailment to all, commonly known as being 'shit faced'; and that she was - big time. And probably suffering from a bit of hypothermia to wrap it all off. As I fireman-lifted her over my shoulder back to my room in the mess I was angry with her for cutting short what was becoming a good night but also a bit concerned about her condition. After wrapping her in my exercise warm kit and my quilt and forcing her to drink numerous sweet teas she started to come around but was still very drunk. She went to the toilet and had been gone for a while when I heard a knock on my door and was told that Catherine was in the room of one of the guys - naked. When I went to check I found her teetering on one leg, naked, trying to get into my next door neighbour's bed. Thank God he was still at the party. For the second time that night I carried her back to my bed, this time locking the door to stop her wandering.

As I woke the next morning I felt her staring at me. I was still very angry with her and I said nothing. After a while she mumbled quietly, "You don't love me any more, do you?" I just started laughing; I never could stay angry with her for long. We started talking and sat on the mess balcony reminiscing about last night, not that she could remember a lot of it. All of a sudden, she screamed and jumped up, sprinting down the corridor. She had put the bath on about half an hour earlier and had forgotten about it. The scene was something from Louisiana. As well as the whole top floor flooded, including the RSM's room, which had guests in it, the water was cascading down the main stairway towards the mess bar and dining area. If I wasn't bust now I would never be. It took most of that day to clean up the mess.

I was coming to my last six months as platoon sergeant within the battalion and unusually I was given the choice of three jobs away from the unit. Normally you were told where you were going and that was that. The first was a platoon sergeant's job at Bassingbourne where I had started my army career; the second was at one of the army careers offices around our recruitment area; and the last offer was as a permanent staff instructor with a Territorial Army Company based in the city of Lincoln. I knew the guy who was finishing his time there and he informed me this was the job to be in, so I opted for Lincoln. My start date at Lincoln was not to be for a further six months so the CO got me in his office and offered me a six-month detachment back to Belize. All my Christmases had come as one.

Catherine's reaction when I gave her the news was one of shock and as she ran into the toilet and sobbed I realized I was not actually as happy about going as I had thought. Damn this woman, she was turning me into a puff! Normally, I wouldn't have given a damn about a woman's thoughts. I told Catherine it would go quickly and she could come and visit me. I felt as if I was going to prison. I knew things were going really well between us and no matter how much I tried to make it sound like a good thing it takes a lot to ask someone you have not long met to wait for six months as you go gallivanting around Central America. I didn't think she would last the course but as she was to prove time and time again, she was my rock of Gibraltar. The CO gave me his farewell speech and I was off.

This was my third posting to Belize and as I flew into Belize International Airport, having stayed the night in Miami in a five-star hotel, I felt like I was coming home. I loved the jungle, and Belize had to be the best posting the British Army had left. As we made the final approach I looked out the window at the crystal-clear waters that stretched out towards the cays and the barrier reef that shielded Belize and smiled, I was glad to be back, even though I would miss Catherine deeply.

The training team had really taken off and there were ten of us as permanent staff instead of the four there used to be. I was also to be housed in the Sergeants Mess, which was a bit plush compared to the last time I was here. With the commitment the army had to throw at Afghanistan and Iraq most of the planned exercises were cancelled and we found ourselves deploying to the jungle areas and rebuilding old training camps and finding new areas for possible future exercises. Life wasn't as busy as the last time I was here and our main responsibility was to provide survival training for the flight crews that rotated through Belize and short courses for the Belize Defence Force. Weekends were spent out on the many cays with lazy days rocking in beach hammocks and drinking local cocktails as well as the local beer. The adventure training island had a permanent dive instructor who found himself redundant with no exercising troops coming through, so we all booked ourselves onto the open water dive course.

On day one we spent the morning in the classroom doing the mandatory theory work before donning our scuba kit and heading out to the reef for our first dive. The water was like nothing else I had encountered and as we sank below the surface it was like entering a different world. Visibility was about a hundred feet and the colours and numbers of the fish were amazing. We spent the next week going deeper and staying down longer as we swam with everything from giant turtles to huge grey sharks, that we were reliably informed were friendly. Friendly? It's like saying that a gun isn't dangerous until its loaded and in somebody's hands. These monsters were over ten feet long and had teeth and we were swimming in their living room. The next best thing we did during this diving week was go night diving. As the boat took us out to the reef and we lowered ourselves over the side into the black forbidding water, our imaginations ran wild. With powerful underwater torches we dropped down to the sandy bottom sixty feet below the surface and watched the alien world around us. Lobsters walked uncaringly past us and brightly-coloured fish moved with the current in a deep sleep. Sleep! I never knew fish slept and here they all were among the coral of the reef fast asleep. Crazy!

Catherine came across for a week soon after that and I went to pick her up at the airport. She made her exit from the plane with her multi-coloured long skirt and no shoes. Be warned Belize, a crazy woman had arrived. We only had a week and I wanted to show her everything there was to see in and around Belize. The country is amazing and we made our way island-hopping across all the small cays, which were like something out of a Sandals holiday brochure, to the ancient Mayan ruins nestled deep within the jungle interior of the country. I took her walking through some of the training area footpaths that meandered through the jungle canopy and down to the crystal clear Macal River where we had a

BBQ lunch and then stopped off at some of the local villages on our way back so she could see how the local Creoles and Mayans lived. We stayed at Banana Bank Lodge where as we came out of the jungle fringes we were greeted by manicured grasslands and herds of wild deer and groomed horses roaming freely. It was a piece of unbelievable beauty that was surreal. The week went by too fast and with deep sadness we said our goodbyes and Catherine flew back to the UK with two months still left to go on my tour.

On my return from Belize I was off for a couple of weeks leave and then it was reporting time with the Territorial Army Company in Lincoln. My first day of work at Lincoln was an eye opener. As I pulled up at the main gates I was greeted by an old grey-haired man who appeared to be someone's grandfather dressed in military combats. He was the caretaker and a corporal in the TA. I drove into the camp and introduced myself to my new boss who went by the title of Permanent Staff Administrational Officer (PSAO). He was an ex-RSM from the Royal Artillery and as he sat me down and offered me a brew his two big questions were if I played golf or fantasy football? I hated football and couldn't see the point in golf so his interest in me dropped fairly quickly. I was asked to leave his office and report to the permanent staff instructor (PSI). He was an old battalion acquaintance, WOII Slater, or 'Sexy Slats' as we called him. God knows why, there was nothing sexy about him. I had worked with him as a private soldier in Canada when he was a corporal and from the way he talked to me he obviously thought I was still a private soldier. I decided that as he had only two weeks left in this job I would bite my lip and wait for his replacement, a guy called John Limb, whom I had worked with before in the Reece Platoon, and was a good guy.

As there was no accommodation for me in the area I was offered civilian housing for my two-year posting with the Territorial Army. My first choice was a run-down student flat in the centre of Lincoln which I refused outright as it was a dump but the second address was amazing, situated in a place called Skellingthorpe, three miles outside Lincoln. It was a two-bedroom Barratt-type house with a garden and a garage and I paid no bills and received £460 a month added to my wages for food. For that much money I could eat out every night and still have change. Not that I was bothered. I immediately ordered the full Sky package and the top of the range broadband Internet.

I turned up for my first day of work with the normal attitude, first impressions count. My uniform was starched to perfection and I was early. I should have known something was wrong when no one was there to open the front gate for me. I sat in my car for an hour until that same little old man came out and let me in. At about nine o'clock when the rest of the gang turned up they looked at me as if I was made out of cheese. Everyone was in jeans and T-shirt and I was told to go home and get changed accordingly. This was to be my dress code for the next two years, I wore uniform only on Tuesday nights and weekends or when away on exercise. It was like being back in Civvie Street - but we had guns.

I was also told not to be too keen and green, for want of a better word, with the Territorial guys. After all, they were civilians who did this for a hobby. If they got pissed off they would not turn up; that was the nature of the beast we were dealing with. The first Tuesday drill night I informed them we were going for a run and then would wrap up the evening with a military lesson and ending with a few beers in the bar afterwards. I may as well have told them I was sleeping with their mothers. They all went into shock and said this is not what they wanted to do and would not come back. The next few weeks, true to their word they didn't show up. It took a couple of months before they realized I was here to stay and started drifting back in with their sports kit.

I enjoyed my time with the TA and the guys, I am sure, liked me being there. I was not here to chill and I encouraged them all to start acting like soldiers. Some of these guys that turned up had their own civilian companies and were not short on cash. They would pull up in their flash cars and change into their uniforms and then be ordered around by me. After one particular exercise in the bleak hills of Otterburn, near Newcastle, I told all the company to strip down their weapons before getting on the bus for the return journey to Lincoln. The OC and CSM came to me with their weapons stripped and ready for inspection, this would never have happened back in the battalion.

I had not been at Lincoln very long when I received a call from the battalion asking if I would like to go to Australia on a sky-diving expedition. It would cost next to nothing and we would be there for three weeks. I agreed straight away. I had never wanted to sky dive but I had always wanted to go to Australia. With bags packed and a very disapproving wave from Catherine, who only a few weeks earlier had done a tandem sky dive for charity, I was off. The officer who had been placed in charge of the expedition had messed up the funding already and all eight of us found ourselves reaching deep into our pockets for extra cash to make it all work.

As we arrived at Brisbane International Airport there were eight very excited faces as we loaded up our bags into our hire cars and headed three hours inland to a place called Toogooloowah. Kangaroos bounded alongside all the roads and parrots flew through the sky; this place was incredible. We set ourselves up in a small bed-and-breakfast a couple of kilometres away from the drop zone and headed for the first day's training. Before they would let us throw ourselves to our deaths from 14,000 feet we had to undergo a day's ground training. This was done with us laid on little roller boards learning the art of arching our backs and reaching for our pull cords, which was vital if we were to land in one piece after our jumps. By the end of the day our backs were in bits from all the ground work and we all were looking forward to heading into the small outback town and acquainting ourselves with the local Australians.

They were a friendly enough group of characters and all seemed like extras from *Neighbours*. At the back of the pub was a makeshift boxing ring. This was for if anybody had an argument; they would be encouraged to sort it out in the ring. What a great idea! Many a night would be spent drinking in there. The best thing of all was England had just won the rugby world cup so we gave all the Aussies we met a hard time.

My first jump was the next morning and I was the second lift up. As I stood watching the first aircraft get to 14,000 feet and start dropping its load of enthusiastic jumpers I felt physically sick. This was not my idea of fun. Even as I watched, a jumper had a main chute malfunction and had to cut it away, deploying her much smaller emergency chute to save her life. The plane landed and everyone ran to get on board, everyone that is except me. I felt like a convict on death row making my way to the electric chair. With seventeen jumpers and a handful of instructors crammed on board the small plane, we were piled in like sardines. Everyone was hollering and giving each other high fives in excitement. Were these people mad? We were all going to die! As we approached 14,000 feet it felt as if we were in orbit in space it was so high up; everything below us were small black dots. On the green light the first lot of jumpers threw themselves out of the door and plummeted groundward with big cheesy grins on their faces. Before I knew it only two instructors and I were left. I knew I had to jump and I also knew I had never been as scared as I was right now. I crawled towards the open door but even with both hands wrapped like a vice around the door frame I didn't dare look down. The instructor grabbed hold of me and nodded for me to jump. Like a lemming at the edge of a cliff, I jumped.

We had been taught that once we had jumped to arch our backs and try and look up but as I left the safety of the aircraft and started my death plunge I panicked and clawed at the air like a lunatic. All my ground training had left my head through my arse and as I plummeted through 3,000 feet I tried frantically to find my pull cord for my chute. The more I tried to locate the cord the more I lost control and eventually the instructor realized he had a complete prat before him and pulled my cord for me. The force of the chute opening and the abrupt slowing of my descent moved my testicles from their normal comfortable resting position to my throat, the adrenalin of my death plunge numbing the pain of their movement.

As my racing heart rate started to come down I finally opened my eyes and had a look around me. I was about 2,000 feet up and it was actually quite a nice feeling. I pulled on the direction cords and started a lazy circle looking for the drop zone. My training, which had long deserted me, slowly returned and I lined myself up for the landing. It all looked straightforward - except for the huge tree that was in a direct line between me and my destination. As I glided down under the 500 foot mark, which is where we were not supposed to make any direction changes, I lined myself up and hoped I would miss the tree, or somebody would get a chain saw and chop the bloody thing down before I got there. As it was I hit it smack on and after bouncing off a few branches I eventually hit the ground, shaken but not dead; and seemingly not broken.

I did three more jumps over the next few days but when my instructor said I was to jump for the fifth time by myself and would launch out of the aircraft door backwards I duly informed him to go to hell. The next morning as everyone jumped onto the transport for the drop zone I made my way to the train station and bought a two-week ticket which allowed me to travel down the Gold Coast to Sydney and northwards up to Cairns. It was an amazing two weeks and it brought home to me the beauty and size of this amazing country. I returned on the last day of their jumps and after a final farewell piss-up that night we boarded the plane back to the UK.

The next year we went to Gibraltar for our annual camp and as expected the TA guys came in their droves. They weren't stupid. Last year's annual exercise was up north in Otterburn and was cold, wet and miserable. Not many turned up. If the weather was bad or it was going to be a demanding exercise they would make their excuses and not turn up but this was sold to them as fun in the sun with a bit of work. Over ninety percent of the battalion put their names down to go. I was told I would be used as an adventure training instructor and would not be used on the military training package that was being organized for the guys. With a hesitant smile I went home and started packing my swimwear. My Belizean lie had followed me yet again and I had carried it too far now to admit to anyone I had no qualifications.

As we came in to land on the tiny Gibraltar runway I glimpsed my first view of the small beach I would be plying my wind surfing trade on for the next two weeks, small and cosy with plenty of room for soaking up the Spanish sun. My lesson plan was still in my mind from my bluffing days in Belize so daily I would walk down to the beach with my TA students, my day sack stuffed with a change of clothes to go on the piss with after lunch. The guys had four hours a day to get the hang of sailing and then by mid-day I would take them on a pub crawl around the small enclave. It was an ace two weeks and as we boarded the homeward bound trip to the UK at the end of the exercise I was bronzed up and boozed up to the eye balls. I had even managed a weekend up the coast of Spain to see my sister.

Gibraltar was to be my last big excursion with the TA and with a couple of months left to go before my return to the battalion I was promoted to Colour Sergeant and given my next post as Company Quarter Master Sergeant for C Company. A life of paperwork beckoned me.

By this time, Catherine and I were well into the final preparations for our upcoming wedding, which was to be held on the fifth of November. My sister had come across from Spain dressed in a summer short dress and spent the remainder of her stay shivering and covered in goose bumps. I did the normal bloke thing and went for a few beers and a few games of pool before rolling up at the registry office late. Catherine, not to be outdone turned up even later; barefoot but stunning in an amazing dress and making me feel like a tramp. My nerves were in overdrive but as she took my hand it all became right and I gave my vows with a lump in my throat. Catherine's daughter read out a fantastic poem that left most of the congregation in tears and before we knew it we were down the local pub where all our family and friends had laid on a fantastic day and evening. The pub landlady had given us the use of the pub and a lodge with four-poster bed, the baguette lady laid on the food, the local Karaoke guy set up the disco and Karaoke, and many other friends helped make this the special day it was. From the cold of the UK we booked a mini-honeymoon in Egypt with the promise of our big one in Cuba the following year.

Just before I moved on from the TA I was summoned to Battalion Headquarters and asked to explain myself as to why the British Legion had stated I was not paying money for my son and his upbringing. I had been paying a direct debit straight from my bank account of over £300 a month since I had moved out of the marital home years before. I produced my bank statements to prove I was telling the truth and then phoned the British Legion to ask why they were giving my ex-wife money. They were apologetic about their accusations but insisted they would keep assisting her as she had no money. No money! As well as the money she was getting from me she was also getting hand-outs from the government, her rent was all but paid for and she was now receiving money from the British Legion. She was working cash in hand at a local pub and not declaring her wages there and getting money from her parents back in Germany. All in all she was doing quite well out of the whole thing. She wore all the top designer clothes, holidayed regularly and even had a car; she was far from this poor woman on the breadline she made out to be.

I informed the authorities she was claiming money fraudulently but no action was taken against her. She then said I was an unfit father and should not be allowed to have visits with my son stating I was an alcoholic, violent, drug-using womanizer who dug up graves as a sick hobby. I was asked to report for a hearing at the local authority's council buildings to argue my case so suited and booted I turned up to explain the type of monster I obviously was. This day I was guilty until I could prove my innocence. As soon as I entered the room I knew I was going to be in trouble as before me sat eleven women, probably all divorced lesbian man haters, with only one token male, who was probably gay. Also there was Uta, my ex-wife. I sat down and with everyone's eyes on me explained myself to my biased audience.

I figured I would go through the list chronologically so started with the alcohol. Yes, I liked a drink but I never got drunk at home and if they were to ask my son, he had never seen me drunk. I had been in the army for over fifteen years at this stage and as with everyone in the Forces we are tested continuously throughout our careers for drugs. I was still serving, and with the army's zero tolerance for drugs I obviously couldn't be a drug taker. Was I violent? Other than boxing or a having few punch-ups downtown I was not a violent person. I had never put a hand on her or my son. Was a womanizer? I pleaded guilty to playing the field but what had that got to do with seeing my lad? The last and hardest question was how to reply to the grave digging accusation. To an audience of stuck-up women I tried to explain the complete story to them without laughing or sounding like a sick psychotic potential mass murderer. As the morning wore on I turned the once hostile audience to my favour and gave the impression of the soldier fighting for Queen and Country coming home to all these problems and I could see their attitudes changing. I wasn't a bad person, just a father wanting to see his son. My ex-wife also saw this change and blew her lid. With screams of anger and further accusations thrown at me she was eventually asked to leave the room. One of the women made me a cup of tea and as I left the room shortly afterwards I knew I had scored a resounding victory. They would not block me from seeing my son and Uta was encouraged to seek psychiatric help. I could have told them years ago that she needed the help of a shrink, or better yet, euthanasia.

CHAPTER ELEVEN

We sleep in our beds because rough men stand ready in the night to visit violence on those who would do us harm. - Winston S. Churchill

MY RETURN TO THE battalion after my two years away in Lincoln was one of excitement and expectations of a good few months ahead in Iraq. I was also looking forward to catching up with all my old mates and swapping stories from the past two years away. As is normal with the army when away, friendships are frozen and rekindled months and even years later.

The battalion had deployed to Iraq two months previously and by all accounts were having a hard run of it in the Basra City area. The mood had changed dramatically in the area and the once friendly civilian population were not so friendly anymore. The company I was to join was C Company, and they were the Brigade Reserve, 'Strike Company'. The job of the Strike Company was to react within thirty minutes to any intelligence or incident within Basra City. We would go into the city hard and fast and kill or capture any insurgents committing or about to commit any terrorist acts. All operations mounted against the insurgents were carried out in a company group sizing plus any attachments, which at times brought the number of people on the ground to over 150. We went out ready for a fight and with enough fire power to win any fight we were in. As well as the guys on the ground, we had tanks and armoured fighting vehicles as well as close air support and helicopters for more fire power and casualty extraction. We also had a Nimrod aircraft high above giving us live feedback through pictures of the area of operations. We went in with a hard punch and were not afraid to use it, unlike the old Northern Ireland days. Out here the gloves were truly off, as had been proved over the last few months with the local insurgents, Jaish al-Mahdi (JAM), the local insurgent movement, receiving a bloody nose. A large number of JAM had been killed and their local leader captured as well as a number of his associates. It didn't all go our way though. Only a few weeks before I arrived, the company had been ambushed with improvised explosive devices (IEDs) and lost two of the guys outright and a further two losing limbs. Other incidents had left other members of the battalion without limbs and with other injuries as well as a few people becoming mentally unable to continue to soldier and being returned to the UK.

It was only eight in the morning on my first day in the country and already the temperature was in the high thirties. Every pore in my body was trying to breathe and as fast as I could drink the bottles of lukewarm water they gave me it was sweating out from my body. During the past two and a half days I had probably had four hours sleep thanks to my friends in the RAF. I was exhausted. As I lay there on my broken camp bed my mind drifted back to scenes of winter holidays and cold drinks.

Then: Boom!

My mind came instantly awake. What the hell was that? The huge explosion was followed by a warbling attack alarm. I fell to the floor and put on my body armour and helmet, while trying to remember the attack drills. I'd gotten about a second into my thought process when a massive jet-type noise screamed overhead. I was to learn it was a Chinese-made 107mm rocket. My head was buried into the hard-packed floor and I wished I had a radio so I could hear what was going on. This was the second day in a row they had hit the camp and their aim today was better than yesterday. The camp QRF had been dispatched and they eventually cleared the camp leaving me to come out and inspect the carnage left by the attack. Welcome to Iraq, I thought to myself. Only three and a half months left. That same afternoon various other camps around Basra were hit hard and a Light Infantry soldier was killed at the Old State Building (OSB), a shit hole of a camp situated on the other side of Basra City.

Being a CQMS was one of the jobs that I had dreaded doing for years. Company Quarter Master Sergeant, a fine name for a shit job. The CQMS was the main G4 administrational representative for the company. The accounts held by a CQMS were exhaustive and endless, ranging from toilet paper to the entire company's allocation of weapons, ammunition and vehicles. My handover with the outgoing CQMS, Faz, began in earnest the next day and within hours my head was aching with numbers and account names; my days of soldiering were looking a long way off. With my clipboards in tow I moved from one ISO container to another, checking off all the equipment and watching my body melt into the Iraqi sand. The temperature topped out at 57° and I honestly thought I would go mad. Why hadn't I become a postman? The handover was pencilled in for four days but as the company was being crashed out so often it dragged on for over a week. At the end of it I was the proud new owner of fourteen ISO containers packed with over a million pounds worth of military kit and equipment.

The company was known as the Basra Gypsies as they were constantly being moved from one location to another. With my arrival there was no change to this. We were housed in a camp called Shaibah Logistics Base, a sprawling tented city about the size of a small British town. The outer perimeter fence stretched for about fifteen miles in circumference. The temperature hit the fifties every day and the tents were no shield from the elements and the air conditioning units had long ago given up the battle to cool the mid-day heat.

The company's main task as Brigade Reserve was to strike at any area in or around Basra within thirty minutes but the brigade commander decided that being based at Shieba we were too far away from the action so he moved us to the Air Station (A Pod), which was Saddam's old International Airport. We had twenty-four hours to move completely up to the A Pod, which proved yet again that the hierarchy that made the big decisions lived in cloud cuckoo land. With all hands on deck we frantically packed all our belongings and equipment and got ready for the journey to the A Pod. As we moved with our convoy we were a sight to behold, seven low-loaders with fourteen ISOs, four Warrior fighting vehicles, nineteen Snatch armoured Land Rovers, two Bedford trucks and a civilian pick-up truck. I jumped in the pick-up as it had the best air-con and spent the entire journey visualizing how I was either going to die by bomb or bullet, or the most likely way, the lunatic that was driving me.

Our arrival at the A Pod was greeted by the RAF with the enthusiasm given to a great white shark turning up at a beach resort. The RAF, who had previously had the tented camp, TDA 116, all to themselves had to move over and make way for us. Where they had been filling the tents with five or six men, we were now cramming up to fifteen of our guys in; cosy to say the least! The limp-wristed RAF technicians were not happy to have real men on their turf and it had to be said we were not overly impressed to be living next to a bunch of homosexuals either. Our tents, although packed, were soon made homely; well, as homely as you can make an oversized tent with crap air conditioning.

That first weekend the new OC for the company and myself were thrown into a helicopter and flown back to Shieba Log Base to complete a two-day confirmatory training package that would enable us to deploy out of camp with the remainder of the company. The first day was a series of lectures in a huge tent that had no air conditioning. It was like one of those sick Japanese game shows with everyone sitting there sweating and trying to pay attention to the instructors and not fall asleep. Four hours into the lectures and the first guy head planted into the ground and had to be casevaced to the hospital with heat illness. With day one complete and the loss of half a stone of body weight, the CO and I made our way to the accommodation tent that for some unknown reason had five huge air-con units pumping freezing air into it. I donned my second thin desert shirt and zipped myself into my lightweight jungle sleeping bag for what I hoped would be a good night's sleep before the next day's activities. While I lay there shivering and hoping that I wouldn't go down with hypothermia, I listened to the incoming rockets and again wondered what the hell I was doing here. The next morning I looked and felt like a bag of shit. I was convinced that Jeremy Beadle was going to jump up and tell me I was on Candid Camera or something. Later on that day, after another few hours of boring lectures and practical training, we were on a Merlin transport helicopter flying low and fast back to the A Pod to rejoin the company, now fully qualified, but knackered warriors.

With my new-found skills of not collapsing from intense heat exposure and staying awake through some of the most boring and worst-given lectures I had ever heard, I retook the reins of CQMS-ing on operations in big bad Iraq. The mornings would start with picking up the company's washing and dropping it off at the local laundry set up, followed by driving around the Contingency Operating Base (COB) to the various QM and signal departments exchanging damaged equipment. As with everything in the admin world there was a load of paperwork to be completed for every account. Arghh! This was not how I had imagined my military career developing. It was not all doom and gloom though. The food was top class and the daily routine meant that I could do two lots of gym sessions every day if I wanted. Every day I would run a few laps of the camp and later that evening hit the gym with a vengeance, collapsing exhausted in my bed afterwards. There were six of us sharing our tent and the air-con worked a treat. With all the bits of furniture we had acquired off departing individuals we had turned our tent into a little home. My bed space resembled something from the Antiques Road Show, but less valuable.

The company was still being crashed out on a regular basis but not to the extent they had been with the last CO. The new CO filtered all the tasks given to the company and if it didn't look like the outcome would have a good result he would refuse it. His idea was that we were here to take out the bad guys and not make new ones. Lots of intelligence came in that was very sketchy and many a house had been destroyed and people hurt that shouldn't have been. There was a Nimrod aircraft that circled the skies above Basra City and the surrounding area most nights, and days as well. The Nimrod had advanced optics and could follow individual persons from 22,000 feet, almost anywhere, any time. If an attack was carried out on any of the Multi National Forces (MNF) they would follow the insurgents as they moved out of the area of the attack to their homes. At 22,000 feet the insurgent didn't have a clue they were being followed until we came crashing through their homes and dragged them out of their beds later on that night.

The Chief of Staff at Division would receive all the information from many sources and crash us out as his Brigade Reserve Company. We had learned the lessons from the Americans in Somalia and as we hurtled through the streets of Basra we would pass pre-positioned friendly force troops manning outer cordons. These would protect us when we were striking nominated 'Alphas' (locations). If it was a high-ranking 'Bravo' (person) in the insurgency, the Special Forces boys would tag along to blow an entry for the troops to enter the building. Normally the whole front of the building would be blown off, making entry even easier. The main problem with these big ops was that everyone would want to be there and the area would be swamped with too many troops and vehicles.

On one of the strike operations I was a top-cover gunner for one of the vehicles. As we moved out of the Basra Palace camp we headed for downtown Basra with over twenty-five vehicles making up our convoy. The convoy was so long I didn't even realize until the post-operation debrief later that night that one of the front vehicles had been hit by an IED. It had damaged the heavily-armoured Land Rover but no casualties had been taken. As we had passed the outer cordon of troops the Warrior Armoured Fighting Vehicles had broken off their escort duties and joined the outer cordon. We completed the last kilometre of our approach to the Alphas in silence. Tonight was a soft knock so we moved in quietly and less heavy-handedly. As we approached the target house, the vehicles came to a halt and the inner cordon troops deployed to their cut-off positions as we made our way to the front gate of the building. As we moved through the gate we were greeted by a mass of glinting eyes reflected by our searchlights. With the intense heat of the nights and a lack of electricity and air conditioning most families would sleep outdoors, with the women and children sleeping in the garden and the men sleeping on the roofs where it was much cooler. Scared women and children were searched and ushered out of the way while the menfolk were separated and aggressively questioned by interpreters and specially trained tactical questioners. These were specially picked and trained British soldiers whose job it was to gain information off possible insurgents on the ground, while the shock of capture was still fresh on them. As I looked around the small area we were searching I counted over thirty members of my unit as well as engineer search teams and search dog teams. Our haul that night was two mobile phones, two AK variant machine guns and a couple of fake IDs. As we moved off later that evening we did our normal hearts and minds gesture of leaving a box of fresh water and some sweets. I could only imagine a company of angry soldiers breaking into my house in the UK, throwing my family and myself around and then leaving some water and sweets hoping all was forgiven. It was a very fine line between getting the baddies and pissing someone off into joining the insurgency, but the job had to be done.

The biggest killer of coalition soldiers in Iraq was the improvised explosive device. Although initially they had been crude and unsophisticated, with the help of Iranian Special Forces who were flooding over the border to help the insurgents in the fight against the American and British forces they were fast becoming a lethal threat. The more armour we put on our vehicles the bigger they made the device. We had electronic counter measures (ECM) fitted to all our vehicles but the insurgents would counter this by initiating the devices by command wires. Another aid to counter the threat was to not set patterns and not to do any unnecessary vehicle road movements. Unfortunately, to get to most of the British and Iraqi Army camps we had no choice but to use the few roads passable to get there. One of the company moves we did was to do a strike operation demonstration at Shieba Log Base for the Duke of Gloucester.

The first packet of vehicles for the company left early that morning to clear the route for the remainder of the company. This was followed shortly afterwards by the second company group and then last but not least the company commander and the last two Warriors. I jumped in with the OC and sat back for the forty-minute drive to Shieba. The inside of the Snatch Land Rover, even with the air-con on, was a stifling 40° and with our chest rigs and body armour it became close to unbearable. After about twenty minutes into the move word came back that the lead Warriors had stopped for a venerable point check (VP). With all the vehicles static we debussed to give all round defence and clear the ground in case there were any nasty surprises waiting for us. Three American civilian security land cruisers pulled up to the rear of our last Warrior. They are thick-steel-plated hulks with big .50 calibre machine guns mounted on sinister-looking turrets. These civilian firms worked on very loose rules of engagement and as I moved to the side of the OC's vehicle a massive burst of automatic fire ripped through the air. All the guys hit the deck, made ready and took up fire positions and with hearts racing looked frantically for the enemy assault that must surely be coming upon us.

As it was, the rear American vehicle had given a burst of fire towards an approaching Iraqi truck. The driver had screeched to a halt and was deathly pale with fright. He wasn't the only one I can assure you. As with all American standard operating procedures (SOP) no one was allowed to approach within 100 metres of any of their vehicles without being fired upon. Their vehicles had big signs hanging off the back saying to stay clear and warning them they would be fired upon if they strayed closer than the 100 metre distance. The main problem with this was that not all of the population could read and the second was that unless you had really good eyesight it was hard to read these signs at 100 metres. When we realized where the firing had come from and why they had fired we dusted ourselves off and made our way back to our vehicles, giving the smiling Americans a few choice words and hand gestures. Wankers was the word that came to mind.

Back at camp we noticed the insurgents were getting cockier by the day. We had lost three guys within a week, two from IEDs and the third from a sniper who was believed to have come down from Baghdad. The rocket attacks that were launched almost nightly onto the Multi National Force camps were now being launched during daylight hours. It was only due to pure luck on our side and their lack of skill that they had not had a direct hit on one of the accommodation tents or cookhouses, which would have resulted in mass casualties. Everyone knew it was only a matter of time before it did happen. When I first heard the rockets and mortars coming in it had been a bit of a buzz, but as the attacks became more and more frequent and their aim better you would sit there listening to the whistle of the mortars and the scream of the rockets and with heart racing wonder if it was going to hit you. If you heard the bang of the impact you knew you were safe, if you didn't hear it then it wouldn't matter, you would probably be dead. It was very unnerving and it was easy to understand how during the First and Second World Wars soldiers would become shell-shocked and mentally lose the plot having been under daily bombardment.

One day we were sitting in the cookhouse, which was also a tent, having our evening meal when the horrendous sound of an incoming rocket shattered the air. The screaming rocket came in very close and for a split second it seemed as if it was going to hit the cookhouse. Everyone fell to the floor and reached for their body armour and helmets while trying to crawl under the tables. What good that would do if the bloody thing landed I don't know. Outside, there was a massive explosion as the warhead detonated, not very far away at all. Tony, one of the platoon sergeants from the company all of a sudden shouted out in pain for a medic. We all looked across at him in confusion and saw him holding his back. I crawled toward him as fast as I could, ready to expect the worst. When it became apparent as to what had happened to him everyone fell about in hysterical laughter. As he had fallen to the floor he had knocked over a cup of tea from the table above him, with the explosion outside and the hot burning tea on his back he thought he had been hit by shrapnel. All the corps and civvies in the cookhouse must have thought we had lost our minds, a bunch of infantry lunatics laughing their heads off as the rockets came in.

Other than the daily attacks, life in camp had become stagnant and repetitive. Once a week I would turn up for the camp RSM's brief along with a few other dodgy characters from various units. They would all sit there with their bulging bellies and talking about what functions would be held in their bars over the coming days and weeks ahead. I was left in no doubt that as the Infantry Company Group in their camp we were the outsiders. One of the many stupid and unfair rules was the alcohol rule. As with all infantry units in Iraq we were on a dry tour and could not drink any alcohol at all. The RAF and many other sub-units were on what was commonly referred to as the non-enforced two-can rule. If you were not on duty and had a clear twelve hours ahead of you it meant you were allowed to have two cans of beer within a twenty-four hour period. By the sounds of the singing and dancing coming from the main bar in the camp where we were staying, this was obviously not enforced.

As it was an operational tour the closest thing we brought to civvie clothing was a track suit for the gym. Nevertheless, our friends in the RAF and elsewhere would dress as if they were going out for a rave night in Ibiza. It's not very good for morale when you are standing at the bar in your combats drinking a can of coke and there are women in miniskirts dancing around with pissed-up REMFs in their GAP gear chasing around after them. Another bone rule was you had to carry around your body armour and helmet wherever you went as if it was a pet or something. This was in case you were caught out in an indirect fire attack. When you went to the cookhouse there were up to 500 people eating at anyone time and your kit ended up being piled up all over the place so if anything happened you had no hope of finding your stuff quickly. The rule of thumb was when under attack to take cover and then make your way to your tent and don your gear. The rockets went from 107mm to 240mm, which is a big bastard, and to think your tent or body armour was going to stop the shrapnel was crap. If our tents were so bloody secure then I wanted a combat suit made out of the stuff!

I was reaching the halfway point of the tour before I knew it and just before I went on my one week R&R back to the UK we were warned that the company was to be a part of Operation Salamanca. This was the brigade's main effort for the Basra area and would take place in phases over the next six weeks. The idea was to hit all the bad areas of Basra with overwhelming force, taking out all the local and foreign insurgents and militia, then, before pulling out of those areas, win the battle of hearts and minds with the local population. This would be done by building projects and cleaning up all the rubbish and debris in the streets of the neighbourhoods. The operation was frowned upon by all that would be taking part in it. We would be on the ground for too long and it would bring in from miles around every psycho with a weapon and a grudge against us. The brigade's line to everyone's worries was that we were the biggest and hardest tribe in the area and we would do what we wanted. The powers-that-be also warned that we were expected to lose one person dead for every twenty-four hours spent on the ground. I on the other hand was expected to get my arse out on R&R the next day so I would worry about that when I returned. In the meantime, a week with Catherine was just what the doctor ordered. Being on the edge all the time takes its toll on you after a while. As it was the forces-that-be had not finished messing me around just yet and after a three-and-a-half hour delay at the Basra terminal, due to incoming rockets, Captain Chaos was then put in charge and gave us all a twenty-four hour stop in Al Udeid, Qatar. My five full days R&R had now fallen to four.

As I wasn't sure what time or even what day I would eventually get back, Catherine had decided to take the train up that afternoon and book into a B&B just down the road from the camp in Shrewsbury. By the time I got there it was about half-two in the morning and I woke her with a bottle of wine and an exhausted but big smile. Absence makes the heart grow fonder my arse. At the end of the day it just makes you pissed-off that you are doing a job that takes you away from the ones you love. Catherine and I sat for hours talking and just being together, catching up and making plans for when we could live together when my days in the military were over. Four days were never going to last long but we did a lot and by the time I had to go back the lack of sleep and the excitement of the last few days hit me like a sledgehammer. I travelled back to Iraq with Captain Chaos's twin brother and eventually arrived nearly a day late.

My days away from the company had been busy for the guys but no one had died or been hurt so that was always a bonus. The first phase of Operation Salamanca had been stopped by the Iraqi prime minister as he did not want British troops flooding the streets of Basra in case it upset the locals. As was becoming increasingly obvious, politics were ruling the day in Iraq rather than doing what was right to get the job done. The whole operation was being re-written or should I say, re-named, and was being sent back to the Iraqi prime minister for his approval. Before that though, the Danish battalion which operated north of Basra had asked the company for assistance in one of their strike operations. Dan Bat, as they were known, normally had good intelligence so their ops were usually very good. We received our orders and drove the five-hour road journey up to our strike positions. As we passed through the outer cordon troops and headed for the three Alpha positions the streets were quiet and everything pointed towards a quick night's work; back in time for tea and medals, as they say.

The three houses nominated as the Alphas were hit simultaneously but instead of bringing in the Iraqi source to identify the suspected insurgents the Danes were taking photos of all those in the house and bringing the pictures to the source at a central location. The time it was taking to do this was crazy and so was the time we were on the ground. To stay on the ground in one area for too long was inviting the enemy to take you on, and that was exactly what was about to happen. First we heard the outer cordon troops come under small arms fire and then the contact reports started flooding the radios as they returned fire with a vengeance. The sound of 30mm high explosive rounds being fired from the Warriors was being matched by the returning fire of RPGs from the insurgents. With the rules about opening fire from the inner cordon and strike positions being strictly in self defence at identified targets, to control incidents of Blue on Blue on our own forces, the situation became even more hectic and confusing. We were now taking small arms fire and RPG rounds onto the inner cordon.

The Danish commander was slowly losing control over the situation and our OC relieved him of overall command of the incident. Fleeing gunmen were being engaged by our guys now and the Broadsword-equipped Nimrod was giving accurate live feedback of where the insurgents were. As I passed one of the platoons they were shining a torch onto a sprawled body next to an alleyway. It was an insurgent who had been hit by small arms fire from one of our guys. His weapon had been removed from him and his entrails were seeping out of his abdomen from where he had been shot. Strangely he was not screaming or crying out like lots of people do, he was staring upwards and groaning. I felt no sympathy for him and no one had bothered to give him first aid as the contacts were still raging on. We had no room for him on our vehicles and it would have been a lot easier if he were dead. In the end the Danish medics dealt with him. Just before we mounted up on the vehicles there was a massive rumble that was getting louder by the second, being veterans of many rocket attacks it sounded as if a there was an incoming rocket attack. The ground visibly shook and everyone dived for cover under whatever they could find. It was a Tornado jet that suddenly shot over us and banked sharply away, its afterburners brightening the dark sky as it headed home, having made its point with the show of force. It had heard our radio transmissions and decided to drop in and scare the shit out of the locals. I don't know about the locals but it scared the crap out of me even though, thankfully, it was on our side. Thank God it was not a rocket, was all that I could think.

As we moved out of the area, the Tornado fighter had stirred up a hornets nest. The whole area exploded like something out of the film *Black Hawk Down*, red and green small arms tracer fire coming towards us and the whoosh of RPGs followed by the thundering barrage of our guys returning rounds with everything from 30mm Rardon cannons and chain guns to small arms. The overhead circling Nimrod aircraft was giving us steers for the convoy to avoid the areas the insurgents were waiting for us and a good job as well. If we had followed our original extraction route we would have driven straight into an intricately-laid ambush with over seventy insurgents lined up to take us on. It never ceased to amaze me how quickly they could mount an operation against us; then again, if you didn't care whether you lived or died it must have been simple to grab your weapon, run outside your house and take on the Brits. We arrived back in camp a few hours later knackered but unscathed only to be told we had six hours rest and then we were to re deploy for our next operation. Deep joy!

A few days later and the Shatt Al Arab Hotel, another British Army outpost situated on the other side of Basra City, was hit with a volley of mortar fire. One round scored a direct hit on one of the accommodation tents killing a medic and seriously injuring another. This brought home what we had all known for ages. We should not be living in tents; it was pure luck there were no more people in the tent when the mortar hit. To counter the indirect fire threat that was on the increase they brought down Apache helicopter gun ships from the Americans up north in Baghdad. This was a raising of the stakes for us with Americans operating in our battle space. These awesome helicopters were built for one thing only, and that was to kill people. Their weapons arsenal was devastating and with large numbers of our ground troops flooding the areas of the indirect fire launch sites we forced the insurgents into other areas where the Apaches could take them out. The whole of the Basra area was now split into operations boxes with likely launch sites being flooded by troops or put into overwatch, and other areas being put out of bounds for ground troops and being left open as killing areas. It worked well.

With four weeks left of our tour the insurgents upped the ante even more by using more and more IEDs. They badly wanted to take out one of our Warrior Fighting Vehicles and daily the attacks on them increased. The Old State buildings, which housed some of our troops, were almost in a state of siege, with our guys fighting to get out of the camp on patrol, fighting throughout the patrol and then fighting to get back to camp. To add to that they were being targeted by small arms fire and indirect rocket and mortar fire continuously, even though a few days earlier our guys had killed over ten of the insurgents and seen many more go down under fire. But still they came. They didn't seem to care about their huge casualties. How *do* you fight large numbers of people who don't care whether they live or die?

The Iraqi Police Service (IPS) were not only corrupt but were actively helping the insurgents and in many cases actually carrying out the attacks against us themselves. Why did we equip these insurgents in police uniforms? On most of the incident reports soldiers were reporting IPS at the scene stopping traffic before an attack, flashing their headlights to warn the insurgents of approaching British soldiers and driving people away after incidents. In lots of cases they just did the attack themselves leaving us having a firefight with them and the police then saying they were fired upon by the British for no reason. IPS personnel were usually killed when our lads returned fire in self defence. The IPS were actively kidnapping and executing members of different tribes and during tribal fighting joining their own tribes using their vehicles and weapons against other police units from other tribes. It was a mad place where the lines of who were on whose side and who you could trust were being redrawn every day. All we knew was that we had as little to do with the IPS and to a lesser degree the Iraqi Army as possible. We would be gone one day and these lunatics could battle it out among themselves to their hearts' content.

We had come here under the lame excuse that we were giving the country back to the Iraqi people by forming a stable and democratic society. What was actually happening was we were fuelling the insurgency and making a volatile country even more volatile, unsafe and unstable than it had ever been under Saddam. All the big players out here were raking in vast amounts of money, like KBR, who supplied all our catering and accommodation. They were owned by Halliburton who also had all the big oil contracts in Iraq and whose former chairman was now the Vice President of the USA. The civilian contractors had massive contracts paid for by the British Government, which included the security for the oil refineries. Lots of them were housed in British camps and ate in our cookhouses and if they were in a contact we would be called to go in and assist them. Politics and money was what this whole thing was about.

About four months earlier there had been a big song and dance about an Iraqi district called Al Amara. It had been vacated by the Brits and handed back to the full control of the Iraqi Army and Police. Other districts had followed this example including the Maysan province which had seen some of the worst violence in all of southern Iraq. It was said to be a calm and peaceful place now, but we all knew this to be rubbish. The tribal fighting up there was terrible and no one knew for certain how many people had died and still were dying. To make matters worse for ourselves, a lot of the insurgents that had been operating out of that area had moved south to Basra to continue the fight with the British. With them they brought new techniques from Baghdad and also from across the border with Iran. The trouble in the area got so bad the Iraqi Army and IPS were sent in to sort the troubles; the local population went mad.

As Al Amara burned and the local tribes turned their fury on the police and army, British assistance was called for and our company was crashed out. The company was air-lifted to an Iraqi camp on the outskirts of Al Amara, to safeguard it and to be prepared to move into the city and take on the armed tribes who were roaming the streets unchecked. Word on the street passed quickly: the British were planning a move into the city and the tribal elders gathered and said the situation would worsen and would grow out of control if we moved against them. Powers higher up gave in and stood us down, moving most of the company back to the A Pod. A small contingent stayed behind to watch the situation and report back if it got worse. The cameras of the world had already descended into Al Amara and the politicians did not want the world to see British soldiers re-entering an area that had been given back to the Iraqis. The Iraqi Army and Police had taken a sound beating with the death toll being played down, the city had been burned and ransacked and new tribal lines had been drawn in the sun-baked earth. We were gutted as we had all wanted to be let loose and take on the gangs and tribes but as was mostly the case nowadays, we were stopped at the last minute.

Three weeks to go and a patrol stopped three IPS vehicles acting suspiciously on one of the main routes between the A Pod and Shaibah Log Base. On approaching the vehicles the police cocked their weapons and acted aggressively towards the call sign. The patrol took up fire positions, and after a warning burst of fire from one of the accompanying Warriors in their direction, disarmed the IPS. In the IPS vehicles were found two ready-to-deploy IEDs along with hundreds of metres of electrical twin flex cable and battery packs. On cordoning off the area another IED was found dug into the side of the road ready to go. The police gave the story that they had driven by these devices and found them, threw them into their vehicles and were taking them away to destroy them as there was an Iraqi bomb disposal team with them. How convenient. Within hours we had to release them after what was a near-on international incident. They claimed they had been roughed up by the British Army and held without due cause and again politicians intervened and had them released. They should have been shot where they were found. I wondered how many more British soldiers would die at the hands of these corrupt coppers.

Two weeks left in theatre and the pace of our operations had all but ceased. It seemed that everyone did not want the Brits driving around Basra upsetting the locals and killing the insurgents. The weather had changed to mirror our mood, sombre. The normal bone-dry landscape could not absorb the winter torrential rains and within hours everything was flooded. To add to this the winds came in and threatened to blow our tents into the desert with thunder and lightning at a scale we had never seen before. If it wasn't the rockets and mortars it was the bloody weather.

The last bit of the tour was spent handing over to the next battle group, driving them around the areas for familiarization of Basra and explaining what they could expect over the next six months. Christmas was around the corner and we could not wait to get home and go on leave, with big smiles and bigger waves we boarded one of the many flights leaving Basra and hoped we would never return here again. How wrong could we be?

CHAPTER TWELVE

Motivation is a fire from within. If someone else tries to light that fire under you, chances are it will burn very briefly. - Stephen R. Covey

ON OUR RETURN WE all went on a massive six-week leave period that covered us well through Christmas and into the New Year. It was a good leave where I got to see my Mum and my sister in Spain and valuable time to spend with Catherine and the family in the UK. At this time, Catherine and I had decided that when the battalion moved over to Germany later that year that she would come with me. We both felt that to try and do three years unaccompanied would too much strain on our marriage and we wanted to live together as man and wife, we hadn't had the chance to since we had been married. There was a lot of sadness though, she would have to leave her job, family and friends and although her children were grown, she would miss them terribly in the times ahead. We knew we would be back to visit and, as time passed, the family all came and spent time with us there often.

When the time to move came the removals picked our stuff up from Lydney, and with a small bag between us we jumped into our little Mazda MX-5 and started the long drive to our new home. It took three days to get there, not because of the distance but because of the discomfort of driving in a car the size of a shoe box. Every time we stopped for a break I would have to dislocate various joints of my body before I could prise myself from the shoe box with wheels. I would then stand in the car park looking like an old man suffering from the worst case of rheumatism ever seen, until I could eventually straighten and stretch myself out. Americans get medals for less than the gruelling three day ordeal I went through to get to Germany.

We moved into our new home a few days later. I started life as a CQMS in Germany and Catherine started work with the Navy, Army and Air Force Institute (NAAFI), a large shopping outlet that had a contract with the Armed Forces to set up and sell merchandise on their premises. They ran everything from the bars, restaurants and shops. Being back in Germany was good and we settled quickly into our life here.

As we were heading back to Iraq again soon the battalion were to finish up their pre-deployment training with a Battle Group Exercise in Poland. I had never been there before, should be good. Of my crew of seven there was only myself and one other guy that could drive the two Company Heavy Goods Vehicles so as we formed all the Land Rovers and four ton trucks up on the battalion square for the long road move to Poland I found myself behind the steering wheel of one of my trucks. Not just any old truck, no. I was behind the wheel of one of the oldest trucks the battalion had. Someone's great grandfather that had fought in the First World War probably had sat behind this very safe wheel on its maiden drive. This was a two-day move and I was sure that nobody else with rank would be part of this road move from hell. The remainder of the Battle Group would be transported up to Poland by luxury coach two days later. There were over three hundred vehicles of every shape and size and we were split into packets of twenty vehicles. We given our route cards and instructions to drive at forty kilometres an hour, this was going to be fun.

As we moved though the scenic routes of Germany you could see the stark differences as we drove through the old East Germany and then across the border into Poland. The poverty around us was evident and so was the greyness and depressed feeling to the place. We were given a police escort from the border to the training area, their military manned all the junctions and villages we passed through, it all looked very Soviet bloc era. We set up in old barns and buildings and over the next three weeks went through numerous exercise scenarios, some Combined Arms Warfare and some Counter Insurgency stuff. The weather got colder and colder until the threatening skies finally dumped its load of sleet and snow upon the sandy training area below and the last week could only be described as emotional. With a battalion-sized piss-up organized for the last night in Poland the men drank their four free cans of beer and went back to their barns to grab some sleep before the two-day return journey early the next morning.

On return from Poland the final stages of the build-up training packages carried on in earnest. There were numerous driving courses covering all the new vehicles the guys would be using in theatre. Medics, communications, language and weapons courses were just some that the guys had to complete before deployment.

It was with a few weeks before the deployment date looming that I was informed that I would hand over my stores account and take up command of the Commanding Officers Tactical Group. This group was made up of some of the battalion's brightest and craziest individuals and throughout the coming tour we would have people of various ranks, capabilities and nationalities join us and leave us. My right-hand man was a guy called Steve Batty, the most unhinged person I had met when introduced to alcohol but one of the best soldiers and commanders I have had the privilege to work with and just the guy you need when the shit hits the fan. The Commanding Officer informed all of us that he had no intention of sitting in the air station and would instead forward mount us at various locations throughout the AOR. This gave him the capability to work directly with the local Iraqi Commanders and give him a real feel as to how things were going on the ground. To our rag-tag group it meant living rough for the majority of the tour under a constantly changing environment.

As we started our final part of the pre deployment training package the CO and RSM directed that their TAC group would be the team that went into all scenarios thrown at us by the directing staff that had organised the package. They were tense and stressful days where we constantly had to prove ourselves to all the other units and the watching staff. All in all I believe we did very well and at the end of the package we were biting at the bit to get out there and prove ourselves in theatre. The guys would deploy direct to Basra while I was being sent to Kuwait as part of the in-theatre training team for six weeks before joining them.

In the meantime, Catherine had applied for and got a job with the NAAFI in the Iraqi Basra air station along with her son Tieran. They would both be out there for the duration of the tour and there was a good likelihood that we could see each other fairly frequently. I was far from happy as I remember the incoming attacks from the first tour but as each of us knows with the other half, once they make their minds up there is no point trying to change it. As it was the experience for Catherine was brilliant and the young boy that was Tieran returned a man with a life-changing experience.

CHAPTER THIRTEEN

I am a small and precious child, my dad's been sent to fight...
The only place I'll see his face, is in my dreams at night.
He will be gone too many days for my young mind to keep track.
I may be sad, but I am proud.
My daddy's got your back.

I am a caring mother; my son has gone to war...
My mind is filled with worries that I have never known before.
Every day I try to keep my thoughts from turning black.
I may be scared, but I am proud.
My son has got your back.

I am a strong and loving wife, with a husband soon to go.
There are times I'm terrified, in a way most never know.
I bite my lip, and force a smile, as I watch my husband pack...
My heart may break, but I am proud.
My husband's got your back...

I am a soldier...
Serving proudly, standing tall.
I fight for freedom, yours and mine, by answering this call.
I do my job while knowing, the thanks it sometimes lacks.
Say a prayer that I'll come home.
It's me who's got your back

- Autumn Parker

ARRIVAL AT KUWAIT INTERNATIONAL Airport and the RAF's mandatory two-hour delay thrown in as always, this time had the added benefit of having us left to wait in a burning hot dust bowl of a car park. A further two-hour bus journey through the desert brought us to Camp Buehring, a sprawling American camp eighteen kilometres from the Iraqi border.

For those who have never been to an American military camp they would find it hard to visualize how big these places are. To put it into perspective we were part of a training team that was put together to train up to 4,500 personnel from 7 Armoured Brigade within a six-week period. This was considered a big job by UK standards. The Americans in this camp alone had trained over 82,000 of their troops for operations in Iraq in the past eight months, and did this on a regular basis with no hiccups. Their facilities were fantastic and we used everything available they allowed us to use. It cost the UK Ministry of Defence $58 a day for each British soldier to eat and be accommodated on the camp. We could eat in any one of their three main dining halls that churned out food twenty-four hours a day; or if you fancied a change you could go to Pizza Hut, Subway, steakhouses, coffee shops, or use their Internet and phone booths, just to name a few. Their camps are better equipped than most British large towns. We used their training areas, classrooms and live firing ranges and even their Humvee trucks. We are such a cheapskate, Flintstone army.

It makes me laugh when our arrogant attitudes actually make us think we are the best army in the world. Yes, we are, or should I say we can be, very professional and disciplined, but we have nothing on these boys. We do small very well and they do big fantastically well. They take a huge pride in their country and their job and even with their huge casualties and longer and longer tours of duty (up to fifteen months) they never openly whinged about it. They held no illusions as to why they were there and although lots of them don't agree with their government's reason for sending them, they proudly go about their jobs with a dedication that is humbling. God, we whinge at the drop of a hat. If we had our tours lengthened, half the army would terminate their contracts. If we put up the Union flag we are told to take it down in case we upset anyone whereas the Americans fly their flags everywhere, and although cheesy at times, it is good to see their pride.

Day one of the Reception, Staging, Onward Movement and Integration (RSOI) training package for us started at 0530 hours with a fifty-minute walk around the American camp. With their company pennants flying proudly at the front of their formations, all the Americans were identically dressed in either sports kit or combat fatigues and they were singing various military chants. Then come the UK's finest, with everyone dressed differently, from baggy Bermuda shorts to very tight Lycra running shorts, even the 'Cheeky Girls' would be proud of. Manchester United football tops to 'Fcuk' polo shirts. Most were overweight and out of step and the closest we got to a chant was "this is shit". It's hard to believe these lunatics were soon to be crossing the border into Basra and Baghdad to take on the might of the Mahdi Army; I wouldn't take them to the job centre, let alone to war.

Over the next few days we were given the mandatory lectures needed to ensure the army's umbrella was up in case we ever said we didn't know what to do when the shit hit the fan. Actions on, our legal rights, Iraqi rights and customs, etc, etc. We had progressed to a slow jog in the morning by day two and as we would finish these brutal physical sessions (yawn), the skinny scrotum of an RSM would look at his watch and scream that we had fifteen minutes to shit, shower and shave and be back on parade in uniform. Two hundred and thirty people to carry that out in a shower block that held ten sinks and eight showers! We all looked at each other, returned to our tents, put on our uniforms (it wasn't as if we had broken into a sweat) and reported back on parade with a couple of minutes to spare. The RSM was livid, we were told that we were filthy vermin and not worthy to be in the British Army. When the tosser had finished gobbing off we all pondered why we were in the army and imagined how nice it would be to strangle that little shit of an RSM. I don't know if he sensed my intense dislike for him but the next day I was told I would no longer be needed as one of the camp instructors and was to move to Forward Operating Base (FOB) Zulu where I would run a theatre-specific live firing range.

The next morning as I sat on the coach transporting me out to FOB Zulu, I glanced out of the tinted window at the surrounding desert and pondered on why anyone would want to fight for such a barren, featureless and hot piece of land. About an hour into the trip I spotted a lone figure of a man staring at us from the desert. A long look left and right confirmed there was no vehicle anywhere to be seen, he was just standing there in the middle of nothingness. A kilometre further on we passed a herd of camels; he was a Bedouin camel herder and these people would become familiar to us over the next few weeks, a group of hardier people you would never meet.

FOB Zulu was a 250 square metre compound surrounded by sand-covered razor wire and a half-collapsed sand berm. Memories of *Zulu*, the film, were not lost on us as we pulled into the compound. There were four old, large, rickety air-conditioned tents and a small contingent of locally-employed security guards whose job it was to monitor our compound and the local range complex. They would drive up and down the sandy range tracks and warn off the Bedouin herders, who would steal the laces out of your boots if you stood still long enough. In the near distance you could make out the higher ground of the border of Iraq, within sight, but not one of us had a weapon system or any ammunition. Hey, we are the best army in the world, who would dare mess with us. Thoughts of the Chris Ryan novel *The One That Got Away* came to mind. Apparently the going price for a British squaddie was £20,000 and there were twenty-six of us here, all unarmed and within ten minutes drive from the border.

As the sun dipped towards the horizon later that night I watched a herd of camels trudge indifferently past me towards their Bedouin encampment and couldn't help but think what a strange and crazy world we lived in. My dreams that night were filled with images of myself in an orange boiler suit with some mad Muslim with a knife to my throat telling the world what a bad infidel I was. I never did like orange.

My life for the next five weeks was to set up and run the theatre-specific live fire shoots; Ground Hog Day was an understatement. Gradually the days passed and at the end of May I made my long-awaited move up to Basra.

Meanwhile, a world away, Catherine had boarded a plane for Brize Norton in the UK where she would then catch her forwarding flight to Qatar, before making the final change to a Hercules transport aircraft for the last leg into the COB, Iraq. The RAF would not disappoint her either and with her first outing with the winged merchants of mayhem the flight suffered mechanical problems and was diverted to Hanover, her original starting point, and grounded for twenty-four hours. The RAF did put everyone up for the night in a five-star hotel though. Wonder how much that cost?

My arrival at the COB in Basra was a huge relief. Finally getting away from FOB Zulu was a huge weight off my shoulders. To constantly not be told when you are to be released from a commitment and to have no end in sight was emotional to say the least. As we rolled up to the transit camp within the COB, I was met by a truly emotional Catherine who despite my plea of no affection in front of everybody barged her way through the troops and launched herself at me with many hugs and kisses. I half-heartedly tried to act restrained but to tell the truth, I didn't care what anybody thought. Those who didn't know her must have thought I had recently drenched myself with Lynx body spray. A sexy woman coming from out of nowhere and throwing herself at a random stranger. Those that did know her just smiled with that, "there's Catherine", smile. Once the mandatory briefs were out of the way Catherine dragged me away for her own catch-up brief and lots more hugs and kisses before releasing me to my transit bed in the early hours.

The next day I started receiving the remainder of my kit that I would need for my tour. These items included Osprey body armour, which is a huge lump of ceramic plates that covers most of the front and rear of the body. They weigh a ton but the protection they offer make it worthwhile. Added to this was the ammunition which included three hundred 5.56mm ball for my personal weapon, two L109 high explosive grenades and one red phosphorous grenade, and last but not least a Sig Saur 9mm pistol with two magazines and thirty rounds of ammunition. I was bombed up and ready to go, but I didn't yet know where. I was to be a part of the Commanding Officer's Tactical group and the main job we were tasked with doing was to mentor the 52 Brigade Commander and his headquarters which was based in Camp Sa'ad, a shit hole of a camp. Ironic, as it was a very sad place approximately fifteen kilometres north of Basra City on the side of the Euphrates River. The 52 Brigade was a new unit that had been formed less than eight months previously. When Basra City had been on the verge of chaos and with the militia groups in complete control earlier in the year, President Maliki had ordered the Iraqi Army to retake control of the city at all costs. The newly formed 52 Brigade had been ordered into the city against the advice of the brigade commander who knew his men were not ready for the hard fight ahead. His plea was dismissed and as they moved on the militia they had over fifty percent of the brigade lay down their arms and refuse to fight. The remainder that fought suffered 110 killed in action and a further 75 seriously injured. After the city had been taken the brigade had been ordered further north, up to Al Qurna, and had drifted from one outpost to another until finally taking up a permanent residence at Camp Sa'ad, where we now joined them.

As for the rest of the brigade, all the sub units were split into platoon or smaller groups that were integrated into the command groups of all the relevant companies and battalions. It meant living and working with the Iraqis on a level never done before on such a scale. There were no army barracks as we would expect. All the areas we moved into were what could only be described as derelict buildings or barns. Lots had only recently had animals removed from them and were covered in animal carcases and faeces. The most disturbing were the other buildings where the Iraqis had left surface-laid mines (i.e. their own piles of shit) everywhere. These were not places left just for us; this was where these people worked and ate their meals. We cleaned up our areas as best we could but the smell just wouldn't go away. To try and explain to the Iraqis they must not live with the animals and they must not shit everywhere was like asking to sleep with their mothers or something. We were looked upon as if we were aliens. It's my cow and if I want to sleep and shit next to it I will, is the attitude that reigned.

We had always been told and taught to respect other cultures, and here in the Iraqi nation it was no different. All the things we shouldn't do or say were upheld in order to not offend anyone, but you would like to think of this as a two-way street. The Iraqi soldiers we worked with just saw us as a meal ticket and had no interest in anything about us as a people. If they saw us with a Gucci bit of kit they would want it, if they needed anything they would ask for money. We tried to set up an operations room for them, we cleaned and painted and brought in tables and chairs. We brought in radios for their communications and placed map boards up for them and the brigade commander came in and threw a hissy fit saying it wasn't good enough. He had watched *24*, the television series, and wanted an ops room like theirs and anything less was not good enough so we had to take everything away. He wanted a shaded area next to his briefing room so he could sit outside and plan his future operations so we set one up. One day it blew down so a couple of us went over to put it back up. There were over twenty Iraqi soldiers there so we asked them to help us. They all walked away. Never once did we witness them do any work themselves, it was as if it was below them, which was hardly surprising as to these people their time on earth was just a holding area before they made their way to heaven. Best speed, I say.

We would be crashed out on short notice all the time with 52 Brigade as they were so scared of their plans becoming general knowledge they would just basically tell people to be ready to do something on a specific day but not what and when. The brigade commander either forgot or blanked it from his memory that the British Army had never lost a war whereas the Iraqi Army had never won one, and had lost two to the British in the last ten years. One minute everyone would be sitting in Camp Sa'ad and the next the brigade commander would get in his vehicle and speed out the front gate with over a thousand Iraqis in every type of transport available, one time even a JCB digger, in hot pursuit. We would try our best to keep up but the normal score would be that by the time we got there whatever operation had gone down was all but over.

One of the first big ops we did was to support the brigade in a search op on a place called Leaf Island, a five kilometre by three kilometre agricultural island just north of Basra. The commander's original plan had been to hijack a fleet of fishing boats to take his troops across the Euphrates River and start a northern sweep from the south with 81mm mortars firing randomly to scare anyone in the area. At the same time a vehicle-bound battalion would sweep in from the north moving south. This reeked of Blue on Blue and we decided it best just to sit back and watch the mother of all fuck ups unfold. As we left that early morning the brigade commander must have farted and a good idea popped into his head and thus decided that instead of hijacking a fleet of boats he would bring his entire brigade in on vehicles from the north down one small sandy track, stop short and send fifty of his fittest soldiers sprinting in darkness to the southern end of the island, five kilometres away, in thirty minutes. At the same time his mortars would start firing somewhere on the island and the remainder of his force would start a sweep from the north heading south to meet his athletes. What could go wrong? The commander was so sure of his success he stood up at the end of his O group and said if this operation was not a success he would take his own life on the battlefield. I think there were a few of us on both sides who would gladly lend him our own pistols for that deed.

Timings were talked about but seldom kept in Iraq. If it is to happen, then it will happen is the attitude that reigned. As we looked at the list of timings given to us for the op it was apparent they were not worth the paper they were written on. We just followed the huge mass of un-coordination that was 52 Brigade going towards the target area realizing we would probably not be back in time for lunch. As the night became day and the cool desert night air gave way to the daily oven temperatures of summer in Iraq, we just sweated and watched the Iraqis at work. They were a shower of shit and the plan reeked of incompetence but, to be fair, as the radio reports came in, large amounts of weapons were found as well as munitions and explosives and a couple of truck full of detainees. It just somehow worked. Mad!

To be honest, we did a few mad things ourselves. We had attached to us a tactical air control party (TACP), whose job it was to bring in fast air support and any airborne munitions needed, and also a group of guys who supplied us with live air footage of our area of operations by the means of a Desert Hawk, a small unmanned aircraft (UAV). These little planes looked as if they had been put together in someone's back garden and whenever they landed they broke up, only to be hastily put back together for their next flight. They cost about £10,000 for the airframe but the big bucks came from the camera devices stored within. I still remember the faces on the Iraqi brigade commander and all his head shed as they watched the live download on one of the operations only to see the controller bring the plane in to land on a strip of land next to them. Parked on this bit of land was the commander's security detail that was sitting behind a 12.7mm heavy machine gun mounted on an armoured Toyota pick-up truck. They looked all sinister and menacing until they saw the Desert Hawk come spiralling out of the sky towards them like some Kamikaze pilot from the Second World War and embed itself in the driver's door. The two guards gave a terrified squeal and launched themselves for cover, the rest of us just tried not to laugh. The plane was reassembled and then re-launched only to turn to the ground within 200 metres and again crash land, apparently due to a bent wing from the first crash. The third attempt of the day was more successful until yet again on its final approach to land it hit a telegraph pole. The Iraqis who were used to working with the Americans and their multi-million dollar Predator UAVs must have been impressed with us Brits that day.

The Danish had partly developed Camp Sa'ad for the Iraqis before abandoning the mission here a year or so ago. It was basic to say the least but some of our buildings had electricity and air-con and without it the summer heat would have made life even more miserable, and sleep all but impossible. We ate rations supplemented by a weekly quota of fruit and milk for cereals and as the weeks progressed the weight started to fall off all of us. We managed to acquire a few cast-iron plates and a barbell and with a lot of imagination we constructed an outdoor gym and a well-used volleyball court.

Routine became anything but routine as we pre-empted or sprinted to catch up with the whim of all Iraqi operations. The Iraqi brigade commander would go to bed at night with no word of any plans for tomorrow and the next day he would send word that his men were at the main gate and about to deploy. We would have minutes to gather our gear, load and move the vehicles to the front gate and follow dust clouds or distant taillights of Iraqi military columns heading off. Sometimes we would have a rough grid or area of where we were going but other times we honestly had no idea. This made pre-planning or briefings almost impossible and the vehicles held map packs for most of Southern Iraq as we could go anywhere.

One such morning we were crashed out to the vehicles and made the mad dash to the front gate and caught the last of the three Iraqi pick-up trucks leaving camp. We had no idea why, where or for how long we were going to be out so it was a normal day in Iraq. Maps were discarded and re-stowed as we frantically kept track of our route. With the route we were taking it was apparent we were heading directly for the Iranian border. There were no settlements and the landscape around us was littered with the hulks of long-ago destroyed Iraqi tanks from the First Gulf War. The Iraqis were waving us on and the hairs on the back of my neck were up. This was not right. We had placed a lot of trust in these people by going this far already. The alarm bells went into overtime when we passed a small Iraqi police post, the most corrupt and dangerous bunch of wankers in Iraq. As it was we got to within three kilometres of the border and made a ninety-degree right turn down a smaller track taking us east, parallel to the border. At this stage we had no communications through the normal radios and had to set up the satellite phone system to relay our location back to headquarters. To make matters even worse, we couldn't turn the vehicles around as the ground all over this area was heavily mined - classic ambush territory. After a short while the Iraqi vehicles stopped and the soldiers motioned for us to follow them off road. As politely as we could we told them to go and fuck a goat; dying on some lonely bit of no man's land between Iran and Iraq didn't hold much appeal to me. After much hand motions and pointing, a couple of our officers and a contingent of riflemen for force protection joined them in their pick-up trucks and headed into the desert. This was bad practice and everyone knew it. We had no communication with them; we didn't know where they were going or when they were likely to return. We sat in the baking sun covering 360° into the barren featureless landscape wondering where we would start if they didn't return by last light. The Desert Hawk 3 couldn't take to the skies either as it wasn't allowed within three kilometres of the border in case it came down. All in all it was turning out to be a bad day at the office.

As it was, three hours later they trundled out of the desert having been taken to a disused ammunition bunker which they had rigged with demolitions. As we took to hard cover the timer ran down and a few tons of Iran/Iraq war stock explosives and weapons were blown up shattering the calm of the desert and leaving a crater big enough to fit a good-sized house within it.

The days were getting hotter and life in camp started to change slightly. Up until now, we really didn't mentor the Iraqi forces - we just followed them. A decision had been made that we were to force ourselves into their planning and execution process and have more of a hands-on attitude. We started slowly, with a few of us pushing up with the forward troops on operations and getting ourselves involved as much as we could. It worked well, even with our small numbers and as long as we didn't get in the way the Iraqis were happy enough. You couldn't directly tell an Iraqi soldier to do something or say he was doing it wrong without insulting them so what we would do was do it ourselves and after a while they would take notice and do the same.

A training programme had been set up in the camp with the first of our lessons being contact drills and patrol formations. As I stood on the square early that first morning a group of Iraqi soldiers came towards me with day sacks and plastic bags and a very obvious lack of weapons and section patrolling kit. When questioned by the interpreter the soldiers all stated that they were here for swimming lessons. This is what we were up against. I don't know how they expected me to come up with a swimming pool. As it was, the training they were receiving from the British training teams down at DTC (a development training course at the old Shieba Log Base) which was south of Basra was top-notch, and the standard of the troops coming to us was not bad at all. The only problem was there was no junior command structure in place and they relied totally on their officers for leadership. In the Iraqi culture if you were in charge you were to blame for any shortcomings and no one wanted to be a scapegoat. I would find myself walking around the Iraqi soldiers and for the first time found that I did not hate them. They were just ordinary people that were being screwed over in the name of religion and outside influence, primarily Iran. The majority of the Iraqi people just wanted a normal life free of oppression and violence and although we could help them we could not and should not ever try to change them. Their culture is that of most Arabic people and as alien as they are to us we are just as alien to them. How can you get them to plan ahead when there is no future tense meaning in their language?

A couple of days later, we found ourselves heading for a place not far from our camp where we were to finish off the controlled demolition of thousands of anti-aircraft rounds. A week earlier we had spent the good part of a hot sweltering day collecting and stacking all the corroded, half-buried and long-forgotten ammunition in neat stacks, to be photographed and then blown to shit with anti-tank bar mines. There was so much of the stuff lying around we ran out of bar mines to destroy it all and so decided to return a week later to finish the job. We had not gone far when we turned off the main transit route, 'Topeka', and headed up a small single-lane dusty track. The area was criss-crossed with huge drooping electricity pylons and the barren wasteland around us was littered with tank hulks and other bits of rusted and rotting military hardware.

The explosion when it came was sudden, powerful and loud. A blinding flash of light, followed by a thick plume of smoke which engulfed our vehicle. My gunner, who was up top in the turret, screamed he'd been shot and crumpled to the floor, his helmet falling from his head, his body smoking. Everything was in slow motion. We accelerated out of the contact point and all efforts to send a contact report across the radio were met with silence. We dragged the gunner to the rear of the vehicle where we could treat him. The gunner's position was occupied by the signaller to give us security from up top. The other wagons in the multiple had seen the explosion and had reversed back towards the main route, debussing their troops in positions of fire support in the process. As we dealt with the gunner he looked up and tried to push me away, "Shock, shock," he shouted. He was a Caribbean guy and with his accent and the shock of the moment he had shouted he had been shocked, which to all around him sounded like, "I've been shot!" He was still smoking but his eyes were refocusing and he had regained his composure.

As quickly as it had all happened, it all became clear. On the personal radios (PRR) that we all wore I told the rest of the multiple that we did not have a casualty and the IED was in fact a pylon strike. What had actually happened was as we had driven under the drooping pylon cables we had either made contact through the radio antennas on the vehicles or the current had jumped the short distance to the antennas below. The resulting surge of 250,000 volts then exploded through the vehicle and earthed itself by means of the two rear right wheels and tyres. How we never suffered severe casualties or worse I will never know, but the power of the strike was awesome and scary. The first thing to go had been the radio antennas and pods which disintegrated into dust, the vehicle radios all blew outwards and everything electrical was trashed. The strike then burned down the back door, through the suspension into the back two tyres. It shredded the armoured run-flat tyre and left two six-inch deep craters in the track. Electricity had done what insurgent weapons hadn't; it had taken out a Mastiff.

That was the second incident that day and I was beginning to think my name was 'Lucky'. Earlier that day as we had escorted an admin detail back to the COB the idiot on one of the checkpoints had forgotten to move the caltrops, which were basically spikes on a chain to puncture the tyres of unauthorized vehicles entering the camp. It was dark and the first we realized there was a problem was when we heard the chain smashing off the vehicle chassis. Two front tyres ruined and a four-hour wait while the British Army's version of Kwik-Fit got us back on the road. Time to get back to my bed-space and shut the world out for a few hours.

The weeks clicked away slowly and the amount of patrols we took part in picked up, so we were out most days. At least it made the days go quicker. On one patrol we were re-tasked to take in three Iraqi soldiers shot earlier that day when they drove into an area where there was tribal fighting. The area was always a tinder box and made television's *Neighbours From Hell* seem like a kids' programme. If your dog shit in the next-door garden you could expect the angry bastard who lived there to turn up with Mr Kalashnikov. Anyway, as the Iraqi 52 Brigade's second-in-command drove through with his bodyguards, the fighting turned towards his vehicle thinking they were there to stop them and in doing so the brigade 2 I/C grabbed the nearest of the bodyguards and used him as a human shield. He took a round to the stomach and the 2 I/C one to his arse which then ricocheted upwards to his kidneys; the last bodyguard was shot in the arm. We rushed them into downtown Basra and the closest Accident and Emergency where there was no doctor on duty. It was a Friday, the weekend for everyone here and no doctor would be available until the following Monday. Two of these guys would not make it till then.

Later on, back at our camp the CO made an agreement with the UK Military Hospital in the COB to treat them there in order to save their lives. Off we trundled again down town to pick them up. The hospital was the main one for Basra and it was in shit state, the filth and stench was unbelievable. I will never complain about the NHS again. Out the back of the hospital was a pile of crap which included used syringes and bandages and what appeared to be body parts and bloody sheets. Very nice indeed.

In the Arab culture, where honour, revenge and saving face are such a big thing, the doctors are too afraid to operate on 50:50 cases as the family will personally blame them and could if they wanted kill them. What would happen is, if it looked dodgy and if the patient looked as if he would live, they were put in a special ward which was in effect where they were left to die. The doctors wore body armour under their robes and a pistol tucked down their belts for self defence. Crazy. It was like the Wild West.

A few days later, we were tasked with our first joint Iraqi/British Heliborne Operation against the insurgents. Over 800 Iraqi troops were to take part with insertion to the target area by land, boat and helicopters. It was three o'clock in the morning and as we stood on the HLS you could sense the excitement among the Iraqi soldiers. We had practiced them endlessly on all the relevant drills needed for heli-drills but had never had a helicopter to play with. Now as the time approached they were like a group of small kids, chattering and giggling among themselves. There were two groups (chalks) of sixteen Iraqis and four Brits to control them.

The RSM and I were in charge of each of the groups and we were to be landed at two separate areas and converge north and south towards each other, searching all buildings and compounds en route. The area we were operating in was primarily swampland broken by rivers and tributaries and would be slow and hard-going underfoot. As the first of the two Merlin helicopters came in dawn was just appearing on the horizon. We tried to instil a bit of urgency into the Iraqi soldiers but they were giggling and chanting and trying to get their mobile phones out to get a picture of the helicopter as it came in. With much physical herding and dragging I finally got my chalk onboard, sat down, strapped in and finally off we went. We flew fast and low and every now and then chaff flares were fired from the rear to ward off any incoming missiles, the look on their faces was one of pure delight. We had helicopter Apache gunships flying overhead as intimate support for us and it reminded me of one of the old Vietnam films. Once the rear door had opened on landing I ushered all the Iraqis off and into something that resembled all-round defence and got my GPS out to get my bearings. To my despair the Iraqi major who was supposed to be in charge didn't have a map and didn't have a clue where he was. I didn't have an interpreter and in my best hand waving and cursing I pointed him towards the axis of march to the north. We shook ourselves out into patrol formation well off to the right of the Iraqis and with the search dog and my other two guys we headed off on what was to be a very long, hot day.

The area was waterlogged and it was not long before we were waist deep in muddy water heading towards our unseen RV with the RSM and his group. The Iraqi major in charge of his lot on the other hand had other ideas and as we came across the first bit of water made a bee line for higher, dryer ground and well off the axis he had been given. They had all rapidly lost interest by the first hour and their helmets and body armour were taken off and dragged unceremoniously behind them. The major had not brought any of the aforementioned bits of kit, but had brought a small ice cooler and a plastic bag with some lunch for himself, which one of his soldiers obediently carried for him. He hadn't even brought a weapon! The operation as far as we were concerned was a chance to show the Iraqis our capabilities with helicopters and fast jets visible everywhere but the one thing it had not factored in was the RAF. A decision had been made that we would ask for an early extraction once the Iraqis had come together as they had binned anything that resembled a tactical patrol. They had run out of water and when we refused to give them ours they got out their mobile phones and asked to be picked up by their own guys by vehicle. The RAF then gave us various pick-up times with each one being slipped until finally after over five hours of sitting at the pick-up point said it was too hot to fly and altogether cancelled. The Iraqis were fuming and at one time I honestly thought there was going to be a stand off between us. In the end we all had to move another two kilometres to a vehicle pick-up point and moved back to our camp. The Iraqis blamed us for the whole escapade and thanks to the RAF Iraqi/British relations hit an all-time low.

Meanwhile, back in camp, Catherine had moved down to Divisional Headquarters and was chin-wagging with all the hierarchy there. On one of the VIP visits she was introduced to Barack Obama, the US Democratic candidate for the American presidency later that year. Just how the conversation came around God knows, but they ended up speaking about her pigtails! As he left, Obama spoke to all the assembled crowd of British and Americans and thanked them for their efforts at which he received a shout from Catherine asking, "what about the NAAFI staff that work here too?" A taken-aback Obama replied with a special farewell to her, which caused much laughter from the gathered audience and concerned attention from Obama's security detail.

Life in Camp Sa'ad took a morale-crushing turn as we were thrown out of our air-conditioned Portacabins and moved into a set of derelict buildings with no electricity or air-conditioning. Life became just short of unbearable as sleep was only possible for a few hours during the early hours of the morning when all the heat of the day had given way to the coolness of early dawn.

The Iraqi Army were taking more and more on by themselves now and the area was very much in their control. On one of the more northern areas we went into with them we were to see how they were tightening their grip on the local population even more. They would surge into an area with vast numbers of troops and hit every homestead they could find. All male occupants were herded outside and the premises turned upside down in the search for weapons, ammunition or explosives. Anything out of the ordinary that was found would result in the males of that area being roughed up and blindfolded and tied before being thrown into one of the waiting Iraqi trucks. The women and children would come screaming out and fling themselves at the brigade commander's vehicle, begging for their menfolk back. The commander would use this as a power thing and eventually wind his window down and order some of the detainees released with words of warning that the next time he would not be so lenient on them. With the remainder we could only imagine what their fate would be. We felt guilty just being there as the women would fall to their knees clawing at the ground and screaming, motioning for us to help them. With our sunshades hiding our guilt-ridden eyes we would mount up onto our vehicles and follow the Iraqis to the next village.

Lots of these villages were in desolate swamp areas and although picturesque they were poor havens with people living a simple life and lacking anything modern. We would watch the Iraqis move into these areas and rip their world apart and feel sorry for them but the Iraqis would find stuff and we had to remember that although they were brutal with these people they and we were fighting an invisible and equally brutal enemy. When you find rockets and explosives stashed in a house and the man of the house says he doesn't know who it belongs to it's hard to feel sorry for him when he receives a good beating and bubbles his neighbours as well. On one occasion our CO persuaded the Iraqi brigade commander to release one of the detainees he was holding to his care. He was trying to prove to him that you didn't have to beat someone to get information from them. The detainee was told he was being released to the British and would be handed over to the authorities at one of the detention facilities that had a bad reputation. We packed him into our vehicle and took him on an operation with us that lasted all day. No one spoke to him and the interpreter would say only a few words to him every now and then through the day. By the end of it, he gave information leading to an address that held wanted terrorists as well as weapons and explosives.

Driving in Iraq was a game of survival. In the process of avoiding being killed by IEDs and ambushes we had to survive the biggest threat of all, an Iraqi with a truck or car. Their licences were obviously found in a packet of corn flakes as they had no idea how to drive. There was no such thing as an MOT or road worthiness test and as long as it could move they would put it onto the road. At night, if a vehicle had lights it was a bonus. We would be travelling down the road in the right direction one minute and then decide to cross over lanes and head towards oncoming traffic as a means of deception, with cars and trucks swerving wildly out of our way with blaring horns and flashing lights. It was like being in a video game.

Rest and Recuperation finally arrived and Catherine and I excitedly met up for the short coach journey to the passenger terminal in the COB. The expected delays we thought were going to come from our friends in the RAF this time came in the shape of the insurgents with their rockets. For two weeks we had not had an attack and they decided to harass us with IDF on tonight of all nights. The delay passed, we boarded our military Hercules flight to Qatar and then a civilian charter flight to Hanover.

Being back home made us realize more than ever how lucky we were with the life we led. We spent the next two weeks visiting friends, hosting family and basically drinking and eating well. It was a great time but the inevitable return date to Iraq came around too quickly. Delays on the return journey were minimal and before I knew it I was sitting in the front of my Mastiff vehicle heading back to Camp Sa'ad.

The last two months of the tour approached fast and operations with the Iraqi Army were drying up. They went out daily and nightly and their success was evident, with the insurgency all but wiped out. The bad guys had either fled to other parts of Iraq, made the short jump over the border to Iran, or had simply been killed or captured. The Iraqi Army was like a kid on a bicycle with stabilizers. We had removed the stabilizers now and were watching as their hesitant few pedals were now confident straight bounds needing no direction from us. We were under no worries that the insurgency would or even could return to the Basra area. The Iraqi Army was everywhere and the people had confidence in them, unlike the Iraqi Police who were struggling with gaining the support of the local population. The people had tasted what the new Iraq had to offer and they liked what they saw. Yes, there were still isolated acts of violence and terrorism but as a whole the area was sorting itself out, and at a fast pace.

The only problem with giving the Iraqi Army so much authority was they had been placed upon a pedestal where they sat with a lot of power, maybe too much. They dictated a lot of what went on in normal Iraqi life and the boundaries of where their job started and where it stopped were not set in stone. I could see that once we pulled out it would only be a matter of time before they pulled a coup and took complete control of the country. Would that be a bad thing; we would have to wait and see.

Also about this time the *Daily Mirror* newspaper came to visit the COB. They were after the type of stories that were not about killing and devastation but more along the lives of families and local boy-type things. There were the three brothers who were serving in the same infantry company, a married couple who worked in the same building, and then there was us. The story was along the line of the wife who took her son and followed the husband to war. War! It was hardly a war we were involved in, but the story was a centre-page spread and they even had a knocked-down version laminated and done as place mats in the main cookhouse. Weird!

November was fast approaching and with it the end of the tour loomed ever closer. The rains had started in Iraq and the once clear blue skies were now an angry black. Thunder rumbled like artillery and lightning streaked across the dark sky and trailing in its wake came the rains. The long, hot, dry days that had plagued us from the start of the tour were now giving way to humid, cloudy, rain-soaked periods. The hard-packed, sun-baked ground absorbed nothing of the heavy rains and the whole area became pools of mud and stagnant ponds, mosquitoes emerging like blood-seeking zombies looking for our exposed skin to satisfy their thirst. Our desert boots became soaked and clogged with mud straight away and everything that we owned had a damp and musty feel to it. The endless summer of uncomfortable heat now gave way to the misery of being wet all the time.

I had been moved up to Al Qurna which is where the mighty Euphrates and the Tigris Rivers meet and the fabled Garden of Eden nestled between them. We had another Military Transitional Team (MiTT) embedded with the Iraqis here at CIMIC-House (Civil-Military Co-operation) and I had been tasked with setting up a training programme for the Iraqi battalion and the British Force Protection platoon living and training with them. The first morning there we were up at 0430 and drove out to the desert with the Iraqi Special Operations Platoon following to the pick-up site where we secured and set up the helicopter landing site for the two incoming Iraqi Air Force Hip helicopters. These guys were the best the Iraqis had and although lazy they knew what they were doing and as the morning progressed they mounted a series of airborne vehicle check point operations along the Iran/Iraq border roads. Nothing came of it but their confidence at using helicopters and setting up their own operations was apparent. I stood back with their operations officer throughout and made a conscious effort to let him crack on with his own soldiers and give minimum direction. At the end of the morning's operation we mounted back up onto our vehicles and headed back to CIMIC-House, with much clapping of hands and dishing out of chocolate bars. Everyone was happy. God, this place was crazy!

During the next two days I was told to set up a series of British/Iraqi live firing ranges. A suitable bit of desert was found and with the use of the Desert Hawk unmanned aircraft we made sure the area was clear of people. We fired every weapon system at our disposal and let the Iraqi soldiers have a go with our systems while we let our guys fire the Iraqis weapons. I set up some competitions with their guys against ours in short- and long-distance shoots, a forgone conclusion as Iraqi soldiers can't shoot to save their lives. Their philosophy is fire lots of rounds at a target and one is bound to hit. When training Iraqi soldiers the one thing you have to remember, as with children, is that their attention span lasts a short time; normally about ninety minutes. After that they get bored and you lose them. Range work was no exception and after a while individuals would start to wander off and fire their weapons randomly down the range. If this wasn't bad enough they then moved their vehicles mounted with large calibre machine guns and started firing with their CO even firing a rocket propelled grenade straight towards a busy road with many clapping hands and shouts from his officers. When we saw them prise open a box of grenades we knew it was time to mount up on our vehicles and leave them to it. When they returned to camp later we were glad to hear no one was dead or injured. We wouldn't even get pissed off with them any more; this was Iraq and this is how they did things.

Just before I left Al Qurna I set up a small survival training day for our guys and the Iraqis in the killing and preparation of a chicken. We had the interpreter head down to the local market and buy ten of the healthiest chickens he could find and I warned the chef that we would be having a feast tonight. As with my Belize days I did the hypnotizing of the chicken to start the show. This is where you run your finger tip along the beak and a few inches to its front, as it watches you do this it becomes transfixed on the movement and drifts off into a comatose state. From here you could either cut its head off or for effect just twist and pull for a quick decapitation. I would do the latter and hold the body for a couple of minutes until the death throes ceased. The guys clapped in appreciation and the Iraqis were horrified. For them to kill an animal in Halal style they would point the animal's head south and slit its throat while letting it bleed to death; to them our way was barbaric. Whatever the way, the end result was the same, it was a dead chicken. It's a shame that those Muslim freaks who posted pictures of their buddies decapitating victims on the Internet didn't think they were barbaric.

The remainder of the preparation went smoothly and before long the first chicken was featherless and gutted, waiting to be cooked for the evening's meal. The guys then came forward one by one to kill and prepare their own chicken. It wasn't until money was offered on the first person to bite a head off that I stepped back in. With a wicked laugh I took the animal in my hands, stuffed its head into my mouth before biting and pulling off its head, blood dripping down my chin. Everyone cheered and clapped, while the Iraqi soldiers looked on aghast, before turning around and walking away from the murder scene. Word came back later that they considered us to be animals. Oh well. I was off in a couple of days. The next morning, when I went for a run around camp the Iraqis all moved out of the way and whispered among themselves. I felt like Shrek. As it was, later that day I moved back to Camp Sa'ad.

Just days to go in Camp Sa'ad and Iraq and time seemed to have stood still. Operations with the Iraqis had all but dried up. They were doing everything themselves and asking for no assistance from us; this was good. The whole idea of the MiTT was to have the Iraqi Army take on all aspects of training and operations themselves and they have proved they are more than capable of this. On my last full day in the camp our guys organized a game of football with the Iraqi Army as they had done numerous times before during the tour. Some games had ended with pushing and shoving but the feeling had never been openly hostile. Today that was to change.

After the Iraqis had decided they wanted to finish the game early, they started pushing and saying the guys had to leave the pitch immediately. The interpreter stated that our guys would finish their kick around in about half an hour's time and then leave the pitch, the same pitch that had only recently been built with British money. There were about twelve of our guys and roughly thirty of them and it wasn't long before the pushing changed to punches. Our guys only took so much before they grouped together and started dishing out some payback themselves and even though there were a lot more of them good old British hooliganism and some classic windmilling took effect and the Iraqis withdrew away from the crazy Brits. When the Iraqis realized they couldn't win by fisticuffs they picked up bricks and stones and scrap metal piping before re-launching themselves. Our lads eventually withdrew under a barrage of stones to our compound, battered and bruised and alerting us to their predicament.

The Iraqis on the other hand now stormed to the entrance of the compound, intent on continuing the fight. We were stood to and, with body armour and helmets on and rifles ready, manned the Sangers. The vehicles were crewed, traversing the turrets and machine guns in their direction, blocking the path of the Iraqi Army who also at this stage were armed and intent on gaining access to the camp. The Iraqi brigade commander now appeared and called for more of his men to come forward and the situation was rapidly becoming out of control. From where I was standing I could see the Iraqis with their barrels pointing at us running their fingers across their triggers and a shiver ran up my spine. They had hatred in their eyes and it was only going to take one person to make the wrong move or action to initiate the mother of all fire fights. With less than twenty-four hours left in the country my adrenalin was pumping and I mentally chose the first person I would take down if the firing started. In the back of my head I knew we would not win this fight if it happened but it was a bit like boxing in the way that your breathing comes back under control and your mind focuses on what needs to be done regardless of the outcome.

As it was, the brigade commander probably realized that if he didn't bring his men under control quickly and this kicked off he would be one of two things: dead, or on trial for murder. He ordered his men away. With lots of glaring and waving of weapons they moved off and we all gave a big sigh of relief. Maybe I would make my flight out of here after all.

In the early hours of the next morning my helicopter lift came in on time for once and whisked me through the dark desert night towards Basra and the COB and my onward journey home. As I watched the Iraqi landscape rush by fifty feet below me I reminisced on my last seven months in this country and hoped I would never return. My flight left the very next morning while Catherine's contract had her remaining in Iraq for a further two weeks.

Within twenty-four hours I was looking out the civilian charter aircraft window at the green rolling fields of a wet and cold Germany and it felt good to be almost home. For the next four weeks I would be a part of the rear party and within days I felt as if I hadn't even been to Iraq. It's very weird the way life just picks up so easily again.

CHAPTER FOURTEEN

Out of the night that covers me,
Black as the pit from pole to pole,
I thank whatever gods may be
For my unconquerable soul.

In the fell clutch of circumstance
I have not winced nor cried aloud.
Under the bludgeonings of chance
My head is bloody, but unbowed.

Beyond this place of wrath and tears
Looms but the horror of the shade,
And yet the menace of the years
Finds and shall find me unafraid.

It matters not how strait the gate,
How charged with punishments the scroll,
I am the master of my fate:
I am the captain of my soul.

- William Ernest Henley

LIFE BACK IN GERMANY took on a normal post-tour routine of parties and sports as well as compulsory lectures to ensure we all understood what we had gone through in Iraq. This would keep everyone together in a relaxed, stress-free environment for about three weeks before going on a big six week post-tour leave period. This was the army's big umbrella in case someone turned into a crazy mass murderer or turned to drink and drugs to help relieve the possible nightmares forming in their minds. I know that people take things differently and compartmentalizing events for later diagnosis is not always healthy, but some people used post-traumatic stress disorder (PTSD) and labelled any problem they had as that being the reason they couldn't cope. The problem being if you didn't take it seriously and something did go wrong you could be held to account for not acting on it. Catch 22.

Just prior to going on leave I was informed that on return I would take over the job of Company Sergeant Major for A Company. It was the place I started as a private soldier all those years ago and I was honoured to be offered this most prestigious of jobs to finish off my time in the military.

Catherine had returned from Iraq about two weeks after I returned and the piss taking from the guys saying I had left my wife in a war zone as I cowardly took the first flight back to Germany raged on. As a gift to ourselves we booked a holiday to Kenya for two weeks of all-inclusive pampering. It was on our way back from Kenya that I bought a copy of the once-glorious UK tabloid, the *News of the World*. As I skimmed through the pages it fell open on page 76, and there was a picture of me in Iraq biting the head off a chicken with the caption, 'Henimal'!

I spent the next few hours of the flight with a sickening feeling of dread in my stomach. I was convinced I would be sacked. A Warrant Officer bringing his regiment and the army into disrepute. As it was I shouldn't have worried at all. On my return the Regimental Sergeant Major and the Commanding Officer both laughed, and although both said I was an idiot for letting the incident be filmed they were after the individual that sent the film into the paper. It came about that it was a medic attached to us for the tour. He eventually was fined £1,500 and reduced from corporal to the rank of private.

As soon as we returned to work the battalion was warned that it would be taking part in a Battle Group Exercise in Kenya. We spent an agonizing few weeks getting hundreds of guys back to the UK in dribs and drabs so they could undergo the latest courses in driving, first aid, communications, weapons etc, etc. It was a complex administration matrix chart of transport, flights, accommodation and feeding for all the moving parts. It also meant that the companies never had all their people together to train at any one point, which is far from ideal. The forthcoming exercise in Kenya had specific critical areas that had to be passed in order that the battalion could be given a green rating. A green pass meant that the battalion was ready to deploy on operations, and to gain that pass all parts from the lowest private soldier to the huge admin chain had to be working in synch. The unit before us had not gained that pass and it left a black mark on the regiment's name as that unit was now classed as non-deployable and needed retraining. Our deployment to Kenya went very well though and over the next six weeks we pushed ourselves to the limit and at the end gained a green pass and two days R&R.

As my time was drawing to a close as Company Sergeant Major, and in fact my time in the British Army, I was called into the Commanding Officer's office. He was offering me a posting to Bermuda for a two-year accompanied posting as the Training Warrant Officer for the Bermuda Regiment. To have this happen with the time I had left to serve I had to get an extra two years' service added to my contract, called variable engagement (VENG). The idea of two years on a small tropical Island in a training job held a lot of attraction.

CHAPTER FIFTEEN

There will be some complaints that we're pushing our people too hard. I don't give a damn about such complaints. I believe that an ounce of sweat will save a gallon of blood. - Gen. George S. Patton

I FLEW INTO THE small island of Bermuda on the 6th June 2010 for a month long handover. I was met at the airport by a portly captain wearing schoolboy-looking military Bermuda shorts that were a couple of sizes too small for his overweight frame and to round off the image he had long socks pulled up just below his knees. Added to this he had on a khaki shirt and a peaked cap. I prayed silently that this was not the daily work uniform here. During the thirty-minute drive to Warwick Camp he pointed out various landmarks to me and what my agenda would be the next day. It was then I noticed for the first time that he was drunk. I don't mean slightly tipsy, I mean drunk. As we pulled into camp he dropped me off at what would become mine and Catherine's home for the next three and a half years, and with a promise of taking me out for a beer down town soon he was gone. Most probably back to the Officers Mess for a few more rums.

For those who do not know much about Bermuda, it is not in the Caribbean. It is approximately 1,000 miles north of the Caribbean and 600 miles off the eastern coast of North America. It is a British colony and measures approximately twenty-two miles long by just over a mile wide at its widest point. Every part of the island is manicured and the crystal-clear blue waters that lap upon their pink and white sandy beaches make it picture perfect and beautiful.

The Bermuda Regiment is made up of around 400 part time conscripts, with a nucleus of thirty full-time staff, two of which were serving British soldiers. I would be taking one of those slots and my job was to be the pivotal point for all training events that took part in the regiment. There are no dedicated training areas on the island so all major training events took place in either America, Canada or Jamaica. This meant travel off the island was quite frequent.

The most notable thing I found in Bermuda was the attitude! Attitude that verges on the black/white divide and a feeling of self-entitlement by many of the young black guys especially. Bermuda holds some world records, like they have more golf courses per kilometre in the world. They have more churches per kilometre also. They have the highest rate of diabetes per head, as well as the most single-mother families. With this last fact comes a lot of young black guys who have had no father figures in their life and who bring the old saying, 'Mommy's boy' to a new level. As a lot of the regiment are conscripts, many do not want to be there. As a professional soldier I expect to follow orders and when I give direction to soldiers under my command I expect them to follow my orders. It's what we do, and it works. When we try this tried and tested recipe in Bermuda the end result is slightly different. I still remember vividly the first time I was told to 'go forth and multiply', or more commonly known as – 'Fuck Off' by a young private soldier!

I had been there for only a few weeks, and after hearing a commotion outside the company offices one evening went out to see what the problem was. Mackie, one of the JNCOs explained that he had been verbally abused by one of the private soldiers. His CSM refused to deal with the situation so I stepped in. On approaching the soldier in question he jumped up and came towards me, stopping directly in front of me. He was covered in tattoos and mouthing off all sorts of obscenities. Very classy! He then stated that if he ever saw me downtown his 'homies' and him would sort me out. The problem here being that when I went down town (there is only one town in Bermuda) I was with my wife. The last thing I needed was Catherine and me to be out on the town and bump into these wannabe gangsters. It was about this time where I decided enough was enough. I grabbed him around his horrible tattooed throat and with a vice-like grip clamped his windpipe shut. He soon lost the ability to talk, which was soothing, and after a while he even changed to a nice bluey-white colour. I finally released him and left him with a few choice words to ensure he never approached or talked to me again. Needless to say I was the one that had to explain myself to the Commanding Officer the very same day.

Once a year we had to take part in the island's biggest TV show, the *100 Day Challenge*. This is where they take a group of the island's fattest people, and of that there are many, and put them through a harsh regime of fitness and dieting. After a hundred days the winner gets a lot of prizes including cash, before reverting back to their fat-encrusted lives. We would put together the final boot camp weekend and put them through their paces, all the while being encouraged by the TV crew to come up with more demanding and sadistic events to put the contestants through.

As we jogged, or should I say waddled, down to the beach on morning two the camera crews were in position as I hurled abuse at them in an attempt to bring out their inner beasts. The only thing they all wanted brought out was a full English breakfast by the looks of things. We started them with hill sprints and then moved onto touch rugby and watched as one by one they gave up and blatantly refused to move any more. With what was left we marched them back into camp and on to the notorious assault course. I was dubious that a lot of the obstacles would even take their weight.

I had managed to find a dead rat in camp and had placed it at the start of the tunnel run, two large pipes that were buried under dirt, and stretched for about twenty feet in length. As they all stared at the entrance I briefed their fat little faces that they were to move their horrible bodies into the rat breeding ground and move at best possible speed to the end but ensuring they did not turn left or right while in the tunnel as we didn't know where the off shoots led to. Three of the contestants told me in no uncertain terms where I could go and sat down. Immovable objects to all but a bulldozer. There were no turnoffs but the desired effect ticked another few fatties off the programme director's winners list. By the time we had finished the weekend's boot camp the show had a winner and we had become mini-celebs. I still go onto YouTube every now and again to see our antics for a good laugh.

Living in Bermuda soon became claustrophobic as everything you could do had been done numerous times and a state of mind set in, called 'rock fever'. This was the urge to get the hell off the island and visit anywhere that had a bit of space.

Another thing unique to Bermuda was their drink driving rules. Or should I say, lack of drink driving rules, more a gentle persuasion. They talked about how people shouldn't drink and drive, and there were television campaigns to highlight the dangers, but the reality was they were just paying lip service to the problem. I hadn't been there long when the Bermuda Police rugby team had their annual 'tugalua party', a fancy dress Hawaiian style BBQ, disco- pissup extravaganza. This was held at the police bar on Prospect Hill, the main police HQ. The night was really good and as we drew towards the end of the evening people were swaggering towards their mopeds and cars to start their onward booze-filled journey home. One guy could not even move from the bar without falling over as he was so drunk. A couple of policemen at the end of the evening escorted him to his moped and tried to get him mounted on his seat which turned out to be impossible as he couldn't stay upright. In the end they left him draped over the seat with the keys in the ignition. It was then I realized that if this is what happened here then drink driving could hardly be enforced with any real conviction across the island.

I remember being the passenger in my mate's car one night coming back from down town, again we were both the worse for wear. As we came around a corner the police were pulling people over into a large layby. I quickly looked at him in amusement and then collapsed into the seat, feigning sleep. He started flapping big time now and slowed down before pulling erratically into the directed layby. As the police walked towards the car he opened the door, with the intent of getting out to greet them. What actually happened was as the door opened he fell out, landing on his hands and knees. This was too much for me and I burst out laughing, receiving stern and unamused looks of the two policemen. As it was they helped him up, asked where he was going, to which he burped "home". With a no-nonsense order of only to go home and nowhere else they piled him back into the car and with a final comment of "good luck" they sent us on our way. Amazing. Why the German police hadn't done the same with me all those years ago I would never know.

A few weeks later the Bermuda Regiment had its summer outing for the full-time staff. Every year it was held in a different location around the island and anyone who had a boat would bring them to raft up (tie together), and all the landlubbers would bring down their cars or bikes. BBQ's would be smoking, music playing and alcohol flowing. It was always a good day. It was about halfway through the day when one of the guys that had brought a souped-up race jet ski asked if anyone wanted to take it out for a spin. I decided it would be a great idea and suited up with a life jacket before opening the throttle and seeing if the seventy miles an hour speed limit could be reached; it could, and then some. This was the fastest thing on water I had ever been on and even though I was drunk it still scared the crap out of me. As I approached the beach Catherine came running out into the water donned in a life jacket saying she wanted a go as a passenger. With another bottle of beer and my wife sitting behind me I opened the throttle again and showed her how fast this bad boy was. It all went remarkably well until I hit about sixty and did a quick left turn and Catherine decided this would be a good time to not hold on and go straight ahead. As I felt a pronounced lack of weight behind me I looked over my shoulder to see Catherine about eight feet in the air, upside down and half way through her second cartwheel. If I'd had a camera it would have made an awesome picture, as it was I just found it incredibly funny and was finding it hard to breathe with my laughter. At about this time she hit the water and then it registered with me; she can't swim. By the time I got her back on the ski and back to the beach she was complaining of intense pain around her ribs and generally being soft. I pushed her off the ski when it was about knee deep and one of the guys placed a double rum and coke in her hand before some small child was put on the ski behind me and the drunken mother asked me to take him for a spin. You had to love this place.

The next morning when I woke up I found Catherine sitting up in bed crying in pain and holding her ribs. After a trip down to A&E we found out she had three broken ribs and severe bruising. I could vaguely remember the jet ski incident but I had no idea how we had gotten home. The scary thought of driving home and not remembering it was then overshadowed by the confusion of finding what can only be described as a small town's worth of clothing scattered throughout the car. Everything from towels, shorts and bras were everywhere. I dread to think what we had done.

We did more than drink in Bermuda though, we actually did some good training. I visited Camp Lejuene, in North Carolina, home of the US Marine Corps on the eastern coast. As we all know, the Americans love doing big and here was no exception. There were over 65,000 marines stationed on the base, not including the civilians that worked there and the marine families. They had shopping malls, cinemas, bowling alleys and numerous fast food franchises spread all over the camp. They had their own power station and recycling plant on site, but most of all they had top of the range training facilities.

There were hundreds of firing ranges, lakes for water operations, enough air power to outnumber entire countries and vehicles by the thousands. We would turn up with our hired 4x4 Dodge pickups, out of date rifles and good old Bermudian attitude, and the marines didn't know what hit them. Each of us would turn up with a couple of large bottles of home.brewed Bermudian black rum as gifts for each of the marine departments; a bit like giving beads to quell the Indians. Every time we turned up for our exercise recces the first question out was always, "have you got some of that black rum". God knows what would have happened if the black rum ran out.

By the time the troops turned up everything would be in place and the exercise would kick in with a bang. The standard was very basic but the guys were given a good package and did stuff they could never have done back in Bermuda. One of the craziest things they did was choose numerous individuals who had excelled at certain parts of the exercise and award them medals at the end of the package. These cheap cheesy medals resembled something from the Olympics and all recipients would wear them with the pride, especially during the thirty-six hour leave period they were given at the end of the exercises. They would be wearing their dodgy gangsta style street wear with their 'most enthusiastic soldier', or 'best signaller' medal swinging from their necks, with a beaming smile. I have seen guys receive medals from the Queen for Gallantry and show less enthusiasm. I could see these same people thirty years away sitting with their great-grandchildren on their knees with their now rusty tin medals fervently dishing out their war stories with much gusto.

The weirdest place we went on exercise while there though was Jamaica. Everyone thinks of Jamaica as this amazing tropical island with happy smiling people, golden beaches, swaying palms and reggae music. What you don't see is how poor the place is, one of the highest murder rates in the world per capita and drugs. Oh, and prostitutes. I still remember vividly the time I was walking down the road in Montego Bay and a couple of girls came up to me and asked if I wanted sex. "No thank you, I'm driving later", was my reply. To a confused look I was then asked if I wanted a blow job? "You look very capable, but no thank you". Her reply was, "Okay, would you buy me a hot dog then". WTF! How the hell did that come out in the same conversation? I have never been offered more sex or blow jobs in one day in my life.

The value of training in Jamaica was not worth all the time and effort that was put into the training packages. By the time we arrived for the exercise everything had changed. Rickety huts were now built right in the middle of our live fire ranges, vehicles were in a state of unrepair so there was no guarantee of transport for the troops. Promises made by the Jamaican Defence Force for assistance were long forgotten. The frustration of trying to salvage some of the original training programme this late in the day was not worth the hassle. My four weeks in Jamaica was probably the most stressful experience I had in my time in Bermuda.

Due to financial restrictions, the UK and Bermuda ended the posts of British soldiers being seconded to the Bermuda Regiment in 2012. From now on they would hire in recently retired majors and WOs to fill these two key appointments. After a quick word with the Commanding Officer I agreed to sign off with the British Army a year short of my twenty-four-year agreement and join the Bermuda Regiment on a three year contract doing the same job and having the same perks. In August of 2012 I flew from Bermuda to the UK to de-kit and end my career in the 2nd Battalion, The Royal Anglian Regiment, and the British Army.

I know that we are all just small cogs in a big machine but I expected more when I drove through the front gates of RAF Cottesmore, the new home of the battalion. Nothing could be found on me in the electronic system and they told me I should have been dealt with by a unit called Global RAO. Global had told me to go to Glasgow and Glasgow had said go through the battalion. The blame merry-go-round of sloping shoulders had started. As far as I was concerned I just wanted out and the main hurdle was my final medical. The army will not sign anyone off their books until a final medical had been done, and in so doing release you as mentally and physically fit as they could into the big bad world of civilians. With my medical complete and a brief farewell to a couple of the guys I left the gates of 2 Royal Anglian for my last day as a soldier. In the morning when I shook off the cobwebs of my hangover I would be referred to as Mr Oldenburg; a civilian. Well, until I flew back to Bermuda, and I would then be a soldier (said in very loose terms) again.

As it was, a year later and still with two years remaining on my contract I decided to put in my letter of resignation in to leave the Bermuda Regiment. This was not a spur of the moment decision and I gave myself a few questions to answer:

1 - Was I happy with my life? My answer was no. Catherine had not been able to work from the time we were there due to strict work permit restrictions. The politics of this small place was doing my head in as the daily routine of tiptoeing on eggshells to not hurt people's feelings became unbearable. The workloads becoming greater as other people shirked their responsibility and you ended up picking up the bits and watching them still get the credit. The money was amazing, but they say money isn't everything and it's true. Our marriage would not have survived another two years.

2 - Did I have an end goal I was working towards? No. Work had become repetitive and I believe I had gone as far as I could go in the role I was in. I had made some good gains in my first couple of years but I could not see where I was going in the future. I could have sat down and chilled and took the money but my pride wouldn't allow me to do that.

3 - Where did I see myself in the future? At forty-four years old I could have stayed until the end of my contract and possibly extended further but that would leave me returning to the UK approaching fifty. Trying to find work as a fifty year old man in today's troubled times would be difficult to say the least.

There were many other reasons why we decided it was time to go but the thought of going home and starting a new future was too great. I will look back on our time in Bermuda with happiness, as it was an amazing opportunity to live and work in such a beautiful place but the wet, cold and family were too big an attraction. England, here we come!

CHAPTER SIXTEEN

I would not fear a pack of lions led by a sheep, but I would always fear a flock of sheep led by a lion. - attributed to Alexander the Great

WE ARRIVED BACK IN the UK on a warm and sunny summer day in August of 2013. With bags jammed into the small hire car and a very relieved Alfie (our puppy) snuggled up on the back seat, we started the long drive to our new home in Lydney, Gloucestershire. The place we had rented was a small but functional two bedroomed bungalow that we were to use as a forward operating base (FOB). From here the task of finding work would be prepared and executed with fine military precision and within days we would be in full-time employment with a pay cheque Simon Cowell would be envious of.

I immediately put my name down for a one-day assessment with the police down in Kent. I had my mind set that this would be my new career and as it was a uniformed service it wouldn't be too far off what I was used to. The day went fine and on my return home to the FOB I prepared my application paperwork for the police and also the MOD police. Five weeks later I received a very formal letter from the chief constable stating that I was unsuitable for further processing due to my tattoos being too numerous. WTF!

With the midnight oil burning in FOB Oldenburg that evening I reassessed my new direction of assault. I would now try for my security licence. Before I could get this I needed a first aid at work certificate so off I went on my three-day course. Next I booked myself on to a Frontline Door Supervisor course for a week. On completion of that course I had to wait until the MOD had produced an overseas criminal record certificate, which took forty days and the security licence coming twenty five days after that. Aaaarghhhh!!!!!!!!

I then went to the Reserves and tried to join up with them on a part-time basis. This should be easy? No, I had been out for more than a year on the army's books so I was handed over to Capita, a civilian company that was dealing with the recruitment for the Reserves. The paperwork started rolling in and got as far as tattoos. I now had to take photos of all my tattoos and fill out a diagram. I tried to explain to the woman on the phone that there were no new tattoos, and asked, reasonably, I thought, why was there a problem now. Two weeks later I received a letter stating I had passed this phase and they would be in touch soon with further directions.

So here we sit on this Christmastime, reflecting on what has been, and what will be.

I am excited about the future and what it holds but it never ceases to amaze me how difficult things can be. But, as long as we have our family and our health all the other pieces of the jigsaw of life will fall into place.

FINAL OVERLOOK

As I finish my book and look back over what I have written I must express a few final thoughts. This project was for me to put down on paper to the best of my ability a chunk of my life. A broad brush stroke of how I saw my time before, during and after my career in the British Army. Although I have written with what I believe is humour, some sarcasm and maybe a bit of piss taking thrown in, I have tried not to put anyone down. I am a firm believer that you shouldn't write or say something about someone you wouldn't say to their face.

I have met some amazing people throughout my life and lived some crazy, emotional and fantastic times. I have only briefly named a few but this does not mean the others are forgotten or left out deliberately. Like I said, this is a broad brush stroke, omitting a fair bit of detail.

Would I do it all again, hell yes! I would change some decisions I have made or the way I did a few things but I hold no regrets as to my life. I will never be rich in money but I hold and cherish my memories. After all, isn't that what life comes down to in the end, memories.

Printed in Great Britain
by Amazon.co.uk, Ltd.,
Marston Gate.